APOLOGETICS
RETHINKING GOD

ANIL KANDA

ADVance Press
United States

Copyright @ 2021 by Anil Kanda

All rights reserved. Under intellectual property rights, no part of this publication may be reproduced, distributed, or transmitted in any form or by any means, including photocopying, recording, or other electronic or mechanical methods, without the prior written permission of the publisher, except in the case of brief quotations embodied in critical reviews and certain other noncommercial uses permitted by law.
For permission requests, write to the publisher, addressed "Attention: Publisher," at the address below or in the website.

ADVance Press
12402 Avenue 22 and 1/2
Chowchilla, CA 93610
www.anilkanda.org

Ordering Information:
Quantity sales. Special discounts are available on quantity purchases by corporations, associations, and others.
For details, contact the publisher at the address above.
Orders by U.S. trade bookstores and wholesalers. Please contact:
http://anilkanda.org/apologetics

Distributed in the United States of America
Publisher's Cataloging-in-Publication data
ADVance Press USA
Kanda, Anil
Apologetics: Rethinking God
ISBN 978-1-7361194-0-2
1. The main category of the book – Religion – Other category.
2. Philosophy – Kanda, Anil

First Edition (Sold in USA)
Kanda, Anil Apologetics: Rethinking God: 2021

ISBN 978-1-7361194-0-2 (Hardback)

Dedication:

To my father, who I hope to see in the Kingdom one day.

Love *never* fails...

-1 Corinthians 13:8

CONTENTS

Foreword 1

1) A Light in the Library (My Story) 5

2) Apologetics? What's That? 19

3) There Is ~~No~~ A God! There Are ~~Many~~ No Atheists! 27

4) The Crime Scene of God 43

5) The Right Book for the Right Time 61

6) God at War: The Problem of Evil 77

7) Genocidal God or Just Judge? 99

8) Abraham's Other Children 123

9) So, You Want To Be An Apologist? 137

10) Questioning the Questioner 155

11) The Greatest Apologetic 161

Acknowledgments 167

Notes 169

Foreword

David Asscherick

This wonderful, readable little book has two things I'm admittedly fond of – *apologetics* and *Anil*.

First, apologetics.

The goal of Christian apologetics is to remove obstacles to belief in the God of the Bible, showing that the Christian faith corresponds with reality as human beings know and experience it. Christian apologetics cannot *create* faith, but it *can* remove barriers to faith.

This isn't just something I believe intellectually, but something I've *experienced* firsthand. At age 23, I became curious about Jesus Christ and the Bible. I was skeptical, but open. The story of Jesus appealed to me on several levels. But was it *actually true*? How could I *know* if it was true?

Right at that point, Christian apologetics showed up on the scene to play an inestimably important role in my life. I began reading and listening to a number of prominent Christian apologists: Norman Geisler, J. P. Moreland, William Lane Craig, Greg Bahnsen, and others. They didn't have to convince me of the beauty of Jesus or His teachings. The gospels had already done that. What I really needed to know was whether this incredible, incomparable story was rational and reasonable to believe. The apologists answered that question powerfully and persuasively.

The beautiful story of Jesus can *absolutely* be believed!

Thoroughly convinced, I accepted Jesus Christ as my personal Savior and Lord of my life. I was born again at age 24. At 48-years-old, I've never looked back. Truth be told, I've never even *thought* of looking back. Jesus is that good and that amazing. I say with Peter, "Lord, where else would we go? You have the words of eternal life. We have come to *believe* and to *know* that you are the Messiah, the Son of the living God" (John 6:68, 69).

God invites us to *believe*, based on external evidence, and to *know*, based on His internal revelation to our individual minds and hearts.

After you've tasted and seen that the Lord is good, there's just nowhere else worth going. I'm just one of many millions of people who have discovered and experienced this. Another one of those people is the author of this book – my dear friend and long-time brother in Christ, Anil Kanda.

Anil is one of those guys you just can't help but like. He's fun, funny, intelligent, and self-effacing. If Jesus were to ask me one day who on earth I'd really loved and I answered, "Anil Kanda," I imagine Jesus would say, "Big deal, Anil's easy to love."

In addition to loving Anil, I also love his story. Raised in a Hindu context and culture, Anil found himself craving a faith that he could understand. Like me, Anil was intrigued by Jesus, but wasn't sure whether the story could be reasonably believed. Like Peter, Anil eventually came "to believe and to know" that Jesus was worth following. How did this happen? Keep reading and you'll find out.

In addition to telling Anil's story, this book also grapples with the difficult questions he had to ask in his search for truth. Chapter by chapter, you'll encounter the persuasive arguments and answers that Anil, myself, and countless others have found so compelling.

Anil has done us all a favor by logically and persuasively laying out *his own apologetic case*. I thoroughly enjoyed journeying through his book. In many ways it reminded me of my own journey.

C.S. Lewis once wrote: "Christianity, if false, is of no importance, and if true, of infinite importance, the only thing it cannot be is moderately important."

Whether you're a believer or a skeptic, a Christian or a critic – you owe it to yourself to examine the claims of this infinitely important book.

David Asscherick
Author, *God in Pain*

Chapter 1
A Light in the Library

(My Story)

"*Mithai, oh mithai!*" shouts a food vendor on a busy street. Delicious, homemade sweets (meetha) tempt the tourists passing by. Cars and trucks honk loudly as they race along, forming a chaotic cacophony of jarring sounds. Local shops bustle with eager activity. The rich aroma of far-eastern spices wafts through the air, mingling with the scent of incense burning to Hindu statues on almost every corner.

Countless temples of every size and shape are open for worship. Religious men walk with purpose, dressed in saffron robes, with colored markings on their foreheads. Everyone is moving. Everything's in motion. Everyone, it seems, has somewhere important to go.

This is *India*.

India is a land of rich and varied cultural flavors. Although born in the United States, I grew up in a traditional Indian home, which has helped me understand the motherland better. I've been to India many times. Each time, I leave profoundly impacted by her.

My parents emigrated from Punjab, India in 1984, one year before I was born. They came to the United States and settled in California. The Golden State possessed then, as it does today, a plethora of groups and cultures, all looking for opportunity and freedom.

My family was deeply spiritual. The Indian faith traditions were inescapably present while I was growing up. Idols adorned our closets and cupboards. Each Sunday, we visited a temple or went to "*Satsang*" (a meeting place for spiritual discourses). Religions in India often overlap culturally, blending together in a spiritual melting pot of sorts. India has been referred to as the "land of contradictions,"[1] and for good reason. Delightfully diverse, India is where Hinduism, Sikhism, and Buddhism all began.

While Hinduism and Sikhism are considered religions, the Satsang (or Radha Soami Satsang Beas) belief is widely regarded as a philosophical movement. This group is led by a Sikh guru, who chooses his successor before he dies. My family embraced this movement in addition to Hinduism. Pictures of a pensive looking man with a turban and long flowing beard were present all throughout our house. We treated these pictures with reverence. *Satsang* (meetings or spiritual discourses) took place multiple times per week. These meetings hosted guests from a wide variety of countries and cultures.

As kids, we met in our own youth room to eat snacks, play games, and color pictures while the adults listened and meditated in the

---

[1] Sundar Mishra, "Land of Contradictions," Social Watch, 2018, https://www.socialwatch.org/node/10624

main hall. Our teachers passed out coloring pages with interesting captions at the bottom. I didn't always understand what these captions meant. One page I distinctly remember showed a nature scene. The caption read, "God is in the tree. God is in the rock. God is in the sky. God is in everything." I was puzzled by this statement, but wanted to understand it.

Pantheism is the belief that God is in everything and is everywhere. This concept was frequently repeated by the people around me. I was also taught that karma would determine my ultimate destiny. If I made good choices, I would experience a series of positive rebirths, eventually arriving at Nirvana – the final liberating stage of being mysteriously one with the Universe. If I made bad choices, on the other hand, I would be reborn into a creature that would experience more suffering than I presently did. Although India has *some* variety in its religious perspectives, the basic concepts of pantheism, karma and nirvana are pervasively woven into the overall belief structure.

I respected the religion of my family, but didn't fully understand it. As I got older, my attempts at reading religious literature often confused me. Still, I wanted to find answers to life's big questions.

I admired my father's devotion to his faith and family. He worked two jobs so we could be comfortable and well-educated. He often came home late and only slept for a few hours, but still rose early to meditate and seek enlightenment. Dad was a gentle soul who wanted the best for his family. I didn't realize how much he sacrificed for us until many years later. His sincere quest for spiritual truth instilled in me a quiet but strong desire for something more. Little did I know that when the time was right, the "Desire of all Nations"[2] would reveal Himself to me.

---

[2] The Holy Bible, New King James Version (Nashville, TN: Thomas Nelson, 1991), Haggai 2:7.

Confused in College

After starting college, I read a curious quote by the messy-haired physicist Albert Einstein. This quote hung on a placard in one of my science classrooms. Each day as I waited for class to start, I thought about what Einstein meant.

"I believe in Spinoza's God, who reveals Himself in the lawful harmony of the world," Einstein said, "not in a God who concerns Himself with the fate and the doings of mankind..."[3]

Benedict de Spinoza was a Dutch-Jewish philosopher who denied that there was "personality and consciousness to God."[4] According to Spinoza, God "has neither intelligence, feeling, nor will; he does not act according to purpose, but everything follows necessarily from his nature, according to law..."

This thinking seemed consistent with the impersonal God I had learned about while growing up, but also introduced the notion of deism (the idea that God exists but doesn't intervene in human affairs).

Yes, that does make sense, I thought to myself. Why would such an infinite and all-powerful Being be interested in the daily humdrum of humanity? Why would He care about a seemingly insignificant creature like me?

Little did I know, I was wrong – *horribly and wonderfully wrong!*

I didn't love college. I struggled to sit in lectures for hours on end. I knew I could do well in my classes, but didn't care enough to try.

---

[3] Don Garrett, Nature and Necessity in Spinoza's Philosophy (New York, NY: Oxford University Press, 2018).

[4] Alfred Weber, History of Philosophy, trans. Frank Thilly (London Longmans, Green, 1914).

Social dynamics were also difficult. Community college is like high school 2.0.

I often ditched my classes, passing the time in a library instead. This sanctuary was quiet and socially non-intrusive. Books provided a welcome escape – delighting my imagination and distracting me from my seemingly aimless life.

I've loved libraries since my childhood. For leisure time, my parents often dropped my sisters, brother, and I off at the city library, where we spent hours wandering through the aisles and picking out books. Several children's books from those times are still precious to me. I hope to pass them on to my own children one day.

In college, I found myself frequenting the religion and spirituality section. There, I found books on Hinduism, Buddhism, modern spiritualism, and nearly every other flavor of religious experience. I was especially fascinated by classic Christian descriptions of angelic interactions. These teachings resonated with me, since the only college class I truly enjoyed was the History of Renaissance Art.

I believed God existed, but He seemed impossible to understand. Occasionally, I attempted to communicate with this mysterious Creator, but I never knew if He was listening. I believed He was connected to all things, but why would He want to communicate with someone as inconsequential as me?

Could God hear me? *Would* He hear me?

All the religious literature I perused seemed to teach that there was some special path to enlightenment – some mysterious and rigorous process that only a few select gurus are disciplined enough to pass through.

I was deeply disappointed by my own inability to grasp pantheistic concepts such as, "God is everything, and everything is God."[5] I just couldn't wrap my mind around this. Initially, the coloring page about God and Spinoza's version of God had appealed to me, but after more thought and reflection, I couldn't harmonize these ideas with my understanding of reality.

In Hinduism, I read grand stories of myth and legend – tales of Krishna and other Indian god-men. The tales were fascinating, but didn't seem true. Buddhism also seemed disconnected from reality. I couldn't seem to attain the necessary quietness or holiness essential for life-changing meditation. If this kind of enlightenment was the goal, I was destined to remain in darkness.

I read that the use of specific words or chants could enable connection with the divine – but nothing I tried seemed to work. Although I never became an atheist, I gave up on the idea of ever understanding or connecting with God. He seemed like an impersonal paradox – close but still distant, aware but still indifferent.

So there I sat, day after day, in the library – aimless, confused, and starting to despair. My safe haven started to feel less safe each day. God – whoever He was or wasn't – didn't seem interested in me.

I gave up on the idea of ever understanding or connecting with God.

Good God, Bad God

Throughout the history of humanity, scores of gods have existed in the minds of millions of people. Yet today, very few (if any) of us wake up thinking, *What does Zeus want from me?* or *What sacrifice should I offer Moloch?* We don't worry about Baal's demands or strategize about how to avoid the lightning bolts of the Norse god, Thor.

---

[5] Owen, H. P., *Concepts of Deity*, London: Macmillan, 1971.

Most of us are only aware of a small fraction of the gods that have existed in religious systems and cultures throughout history. But this is actually to our benefit.

Why?

It's really good news that Zeus isn't trying to seduce your sister, that Moloch isn't demanding you to sacrifice your children, and that Ares isn't starting a war with your nation. These gods are so selfish and evil that the world is a better place without them.

It's good news those gods don't exist, because the character of those gods are so vile and evil, that the world is better without them, then it is with them.

The world is better off without those gods, than it is with those gods.

We're better off in a world where we don't have to appease devious divine entities. We're better off living free from the guilt and fear they produce. We're better off not having to tiptoe around gods who punish our every mistake.

It's an easier psychological activity to live with no gods, than to live with those depictions.

One can understand why some people choose atheism if this is all they understand. But are we better off with no God at all?

What about the God of the Bible? Should we toss Him out too? Of the thousands of depictions of gods, the God of the Bible makes up less than 1% of the total number of beliefs. Should we throw this proverbial *baby out with the bath water?*

Isn't this God supposed to be *good news?*

Little did I know that I was about to find out.

Paradigm Shift

Despite my spiritual discouragement, I found myself gravitating toward apocalyptic literature. Books on Revelation and the end of the world captured my attention. The planet had always seemed to me to be in a state of tension and drama. Over the years, I'd heard enthusiastic televangelists spout strange words and phrases like *antichrist, Revelation, second coming,* and *signs of the times*. During this period of my life, I didn't know a single Christian personally, but I sometimes ran into zealous Christians who shared religious tracts about God, heaven, hell, and salvation.

My interest in apocalyptic themes sent my mind in new directions. I wondered if I would be "lost" if I died, whatever "lost" meant. Would I have to face some kind of divine judgment? If God truly existed, how would I approach Him in the afterlife? Would He punish me or receive me? My apocalyptic curiosity brought me face to face with my own mortality in a way I hadn't experienced before.

While reading some books on biblical prophecy, I was exposed to some pretty "out there" thinking regarding the book of Revelation and end-time events. I didn't spend much time reading the Bible itself since it seemed similar to the spiritual literature I grew up with. My King James version of Scripture sounded like a Shakespearian play with its *thees, thous, thuses, etc.*

As time went on, I met many nice Christians. From Baptists and Lutherans to Mormons and Catholics, most of them seemed pleasant enough. Eventually and, I believe *providentially*, I started working with a friendly Seventh-Day Adventist Christian. After multiple conversations, we started talking about faith and truth. Soon, he invited me to study the Bible with his family.

As we studied together, I felt impressed that these kind and humble people were actually connected with God. It seemed that God listened to and even *answered* their prayers. I envied their experiences and their unmistakable joy. They seemed to possess something I hadn't seen in other paths or religions. Through their witness, I started to see the Bible as a new book – perhaps even *God's own book*!

My blurry concept of God was finally beginning to come into focus.

As I opened my heart to this new picture of God, I began to feel that He was more than just "everywhere," in some general sense. He was actually very near – so close that He even craved a personal connection with me! This thought was astounding! The Bible, which I started reading regularly, quickly became a portal through which the Creator God spoke things that were intimately relevant to *me*, to *my* soul.

The Bible shone light on my darkened perceptions of God.

I soon realized God had been present with me all along. He saw my restless wanderings and quiet moments of reflection. He heard my prayers despite my doubts. He gave me a desire for something more. He gradually led me to the truth about Himself – a truth much brighter and much more beautiful than I had previously imagined possible.

Often, God whispers to people in their innermost souls before He dramatically and persuasively manifests Himself to them. The Apostle Paul describes this in the first chapter of Romans.

I came to realize that I had not been on a journey to God; but on a journey *with* God. As I continued reading my Bible, I discovered that the *beautiful and personal Creator God was knowable through Jesus Christ.*

Jesus is different

Many spiritual teachers have mistakenly claimed to have the truth. Many religious systems have promised peace, but instead driven people to hopelessness and despair. Pagan idols have been created to satisfy the human soul's deep longing to connect with the unseen.

But Jesus is different.

In the Bible, I discovered that Jesus Christ came into this world to perfectly reveal who God really is. Jesus came as the full revelation of the incredible truth that philosophers and wise men had spent their lives seeking. On one occasion, Jesus referred to Himself as "the door" (John 10:9-16). What are doors for? Access and entrance! Through Christ, the infinite God of the Universe opens the door for every human being – even the most sinful and needy ones – to find access to Him.

The Gospel is much more than spirituality and religious tenets. It is the height of Divine interaction. While every other religion is about man's search for God, the Gospel is all about God's pursuit to reach man.

Jesus is humanity's representative to God, and God's representative to humanity. Christ even had the audacity to say, "If you have seen Me, you have seen the Father" (John 14:9). I still remember how remarkable it felt to discover that God, through Christ, was accessible to *me*! He invited *me* to approach Him!

I began to earnestly pray, asking God to reveal His will for my life. Things were changing so fast, so powerfully, and so wonderfully. God was *real*, He was *beautiful*, and *He loved me!*

Dear reader, please believe me when I tell you this: God loves you too. He has a remarkably unique plan and purpose for your life.

> ### *God leads us the way we would choose to be led if we could see what He sees.*

Unsure of my future, I sought God for guidance and direction. One night, I desperately prayed until midnight, when I sensed God speaking to me in a clear, unmistakable way. I was impressed to look for a Christian school. Soon after this, a friend and I approached a pastor, who told us about a Christian school focused of ministry and evangelism.

I left home with a conflicted heart, still grieving the recent loss of my father. I believed God was leading me, but it felt bittersweet to leave my childhood home. God often removes people from the environment they are most comfortable in in order to stretch and grow them. God called Abraham to leave his home, and I clearly sensed He was asking me to do the same. I knew God would bless me for following him.

> ### *There's no comfort in the growth zone, and there's no growth in the comfort zone.*

After an amazing, four-month course on evangelism, personal ministry, and Bible doctrines, I knew I needed more. It was wonderful to be around so many young adults who loved God and wanted to His purpose to be fulfilled in their lives, especially after the disheartening experience I had in college.

After much prayer and a series of providential events, I was led to a small Christian college in the Sierra Nevada Mountains of California. My faith blossomed as I met other Christians, many who are still dear friends to this day.

I often didn't know how I would pay my tuition. Yet time and time again, God provided in astounding ways. I knew His presence was real and His promises were true. I also knew He was calling me to share what I was learning with others.

Faith grows in the soil of troubles and tensions.

Since graduating from that college, God has taken me on a remarkable journey. I've had the privilege of doing evangelism around the world, planting and pastoring churches, and working with thousands of young adults. I've met countless amazing and inspiring people along the way. I know beyond the shadow of a doubt that *God is real and He is faithful!*

One passage that seems to describe my life well is Jeremiah 29:11-13:

> "For I know the plans I have for you,' declares the Lord, 'plans to prosper you and not to harm you, plans to give you hope and a future. Then you will call on me and come and pray to me, and I will listen to you. You will seek me and find me when you search for me with all your heart.'"

God definitely means what He's saying. "I know the plans," He says. *I know what I'm thinking and I know it's good.* How cool is that?
God makes it crystal clear that He wants to bless our futures.

The truth is that, outside of our Creator, *we have no real future.*

As the passage continues, God invites every human being to *seek* Him — not with telescopes or rocket ships, but in the intimate place where it matters most — our hearts. This is where the real search begins! In our hearts, we can reflect on God, cry out to Him, and choose to follow His gentle leading.

How will He respond? The passage makes it clear. "I will be found by you," declares the LORD (Jeremiah 29:14).

God wants to be found

One day, I visited a Sikh chiropractor to have my neck adjusted. As he performed his twists and turns on my joints, he asked some questions about my life. I decided to share a little about my faith. After listening quietly for a few minutes, he shared his opinion:

> "I believe all religions are the same. At the core of it, all religions are the same..."

After listening to him, I respectfully said: "I noticed you said something interesting. You said, 'at the core of it'..."

"Yes?" he replied.

"Well, what if it's not about an '*it*', but instead about a *Who*?" I asked "What if life is a journey to discover who He is, the One who existed before all things and made all things? What if knowing Him is the greatest of all experiences?"

The man listened quietly. Somehow, he must have been touched, because the next words that came out of his mouth were, "Can you pray for me?"

God desires to be known! He doesn't hide Himself away or reveal Himself to only a select, extra-special few.

No! God is love,[6] and love invites connection, relationship, and discovery.

This discovery is a privilege. Indeed, I believe the greatest thing a person can ever accomplish or experience is to know the Creator.

---

[6] 1 Jn 4:17

I've written this humble book for you (and hopefully for your family, friends, and neighbors too). I want it to help you focus (or maybe *refocus*) your emotional and intellectual lenses in order to see God more clearly.

Many people have been deceived and confused by lies perpetuated about God. This book will explore some of the most common objections people have to God, faith, and Scripture. It will tackle difficult questions, such as:

- *How can you prove God's existence?*
- *Why does God allow so much suffering?*
- *Why did God promote violence in the Old Testament?*
- *Why should we trust the Bible?*
- *and more...*

God isn't afraid of difficult questions. Instead, He welcomes them. He knows we can't love Him if He seems unlovable or trust in things that seem like fairy tales. As one writer aptly puts it, "We can't believe what we believe to be untrue, and we can't love what we believe to be unreal."[7]

This book was written for seekers, saints, scholars, students, and even skeptics. Most of all, it's written for the other *Anil Kandas* out there – people who quietly wonder about God and the things that matter most, but don't know where to turn. Although the book was designed with a developmental focus, feel free to read the parts which interests you the most.

When the true picture of God comes into focus, suddenly the rest of life does too. Life itself begins to align.

---

[7] Peter Kreeft and Ronald K. Tacelli, Pocket Handbook of Christian Apologetics (Downers Grove, Ill.: Intervarsity Press, 2003).

Chapter 2
Apologetics? *What's That?*

"Please rise. The world court is now in session!"

The air is thick with nervous tension. So much is at stake. The scene is one of formality and professional pomp. The positions of the courtroom actors are precisely arranged. Soon, the buzz of nervous whispering dies out as the bailiff motions for people's attention.

The judge looks distinguished in his robe. He towers above the rest, sitting behind his massive, imposing desk. To the left, an ethnically diverse jury is seated, attentively observing the scene before them. The prosecutor rises, dramatically clears his throat, and formally announces the charges:

"The defendant has been charged with crimes against humanity, against the Universe, and against all that is good!"

At that moment, all attention is drawn to the courtroom's center, where a lowly Galilean Carpenter calmly sits. His eyes look sad, but kind. Despite the accusations, everyone in the room can tell that something is different about Him – something good.

Before the accusers, the observers, the jury, and the judge, sits One who has been the subject of great debate: Jesus Christ.

No other name in history has been associated with such good, such evil, and such confusion. From the rise and fall of nations, to countless acts of both cruelty and charity, to the beliefs and values of many people – the tide of human history has been deeply influenced by the name of Jesus Christ. In almost every country, His name invokes deep passion of some kind.

Some people love Him and some people hate him. But today, in our imaginary court scene, God Himself is on trial. The hour of *His judgment* has come.[8]

In this magnificent courtroom, witnesses are called to testify on behalf of, or in opposition to, the heavenly Defendant. Angels are not called to the stand. Instead, humanity has been chosen to bear witness. Isaiah 43:10 states, "You are My witnesses."[9]

Yes, you and I get to decide what kind of testimony we will give about the incarnate God, Jesus Christ.

Faith and Reason

The Greek word apologia was used in ancient courtrooms to describe the action of giving a legal defense or answer. Similarly,

---

[8] Rev. 14

[9] Isa. 43

the English word "apologetics" means to give a defense of a position, particularly a religious one. For example, Peter writes in his first epistle: "Be ready always to give a defense [apologia] of the hope that is within you, with meekness and fear" (1 Peter 3:15).

Apologetics has been defined as "verbal defense" or "speech in defense."[10] It's the discipline of giving a rational and persuasive justification of one's theological beliefs by employing logic, philosophy, science, and even the arts. As theologian R.C. Sproul notes, "the defense of the faith is not a luxury or intellectual vanity. It's a task appointed by God that you should be able to give a reason for the hope that is in you as you bear witness before the world."[11]

The word *apologetics* shouldn't be confused with the notion of apologizing to someone for a wrong done (*i.e. He was very apologetic for forgetting her birthday*). Apologetics is about defending faith, not apologizing for it! The idea is simple. If Christianity really makes sense, shouldn't Christians be able to explain why?

> ***We expect evidence for all the other things we believe. Why wouldn't we expect evidence when it comes to faith?***

Apologetics seeks to overcome intellectual barriers to belief, engaging doubters and skeptics in the realm of reason. Encouraging open dialogue, it explores and explains why faith is rational and intellectually compelling. Apologetics creates a friendly place for people to ask difficult questions so they can discover who God

---

[10] James Orr, International Standard Bible Encyclopedia, Vol. 1. (Grand Rapids, Michigan: Wm. B. Eerdmans Pub. Co, 2003).

[11] R.C. Sproul, Defending Your Faith: An Introduction to Apologetics (Wheaton, IL: Crossway, 2003).

really is. In short, apologetics seeks to clarify the true picture of God revealed in Scripture, the God who is called *Love*.[12]

Of course, this process should not be argumentative or unkind. Conversations on differing viewpoints should always be engaged in with a kind and humble spirit. How can we show that God is love if the way we talk about Him isn't loving?

> ***The goal of apologetics is to reveal the truth and beauty of God's character.***

A New Perspective

Given my traditional Indian faith background, my choice to follow Jesus was a radical decision. The entire trajectory of my life shifted. The reason I changed my mind about Christ was because someone took the time to thoughtfully answer my questions and clear up my misunderstandings.

As I grew up, I only had negative perspectives about Christianity and the Bible. But during college, I had nagging and unresolved questions about God and His character. God knew my need and sent people into my life to help answer my questions.

According to Kenneth Samples, an apologetics professor at Biola University, "Christianity is rarely understood by those outside its bounds. In fact, this is probably *one of the greatest tasks* confronting the apologist – to rescue Christianity from misunderstandings."[13]

I'm so grateful that the people who studied the Bible with me helped *rescue me* from my misunderstandings. If this had never happened,

---

[12] 1 Jn 4:17

[13] Kenneth R. Samples, Without a Doubt: Answering the 20 Toughest Faith Questions (Grand Rapids, MI: Baker Books, 2004).

I would have missed out on the most valuable experience (and the most valuable relationship) I've ever had.

I'm not the only one who has struggled with nagging, unanswered questions about God and faith. That's why I care about apologetics. I believe the complex questions people ask deserve thoughtful, rational, and evidence-based answers. That's why I'm writing this book.

> *Many have heard false things about God, then chosen not to believe in Him.*

Myths about Christianity

Since its inception, the Christian faith has been perpetually misunderstood. Early Christians were falsely accused of being cannibalistic, incestuous magicians who practiced dangerous superstitions and when calamities struck (such as the burning of Rome in A.D. 64), followers of Jesus were often blamed for these events by corrupt politicians, despite the lack of corresponding evidence. Christians were accused and persecuted by critics who didn't take the time to understand their faith.

Thankfully, Christian apologists rose in defense of the truth. They wrote powerful and persuasive clarifications of what they actually believed and why. Many of these writings are still preserved today. Check out the "Apologies" manuscripts from early Christian writers such as Tertullian.

As Christianity grew, political leaders realized their strategy must change in order to maintain control of the people. Many pagan leaders "converted" to Christianity, without truly having a conversion of heart or a commitment to follow God's principles. Heathen ideas were introduced into the once pure Christian faith. Political leaders used Christianity as an excuse for their own violent agendas and conquests. Although the church changed forms and became corrupt, God's true followers still held fast to Biblical principles.

During the Middle Ages, believers were persecuted (by the state church) for believing and sharing Biblical truths. Many lost their lives. Still, Christian "apologists" challenged the prevailing ideas of their time through sermons, public defenses, and publications. Martin Luther, one of the most effective apologists of all time, even nailed his biblical protests on the entrance of a prominent church, despite the risk this posed to his career and life. Martin Luther was fighting against false ideas about God that were being promoted, not by outsiders, but by the church itself.

It's no wonder that so many people have given up on the idea of a loving God. Not only has God been misrepresented by the serpent who deceived Adam and Eve, but also by the church. False teachings have crept into mainstream Christianity, confusing people about what God is truly like.

That's why now – more than ever – it's important to grapple with difficult questions about faith. I believe that the Second Coming of Christ is very soon. Unprecedented events are culminating for a climactic close to this world's history. I believe God is working to bring truth and clarity to people's minds in order to save as many people as possible. To do this, He must win our trust. That's what apologetics is all about.

The following chapters will discuss some of the reasons why I believe God is trustworthy and His word is true. We'll explore some of the most challenging philosophical and theological objections that people have to faith. If you have questions about faith, or want to help someone who does, keep reading!

THINKING ABOUT APOLOGETICS:

- Have you ever had a bad first impression of someone, but later changed your mind? What happened?

- How important do you think it is to challenge your assumptions about God?

- How does it feel to know that God takes your questions seriously and wants to help you find answers?

- Are you interested in learning to share your faith more intelligently? If so, you'll enjoy the *"How to Be an Apologist"* chapter later in this book.

Chapter 3

There is ~~no~~ *a* God and There Are ~~Many~~ *no* Atheists!

Many people mocked Antony Flew.

He was called *"an aging, fading scholar who is severely memory-impaired."*[14]

He was accused of delusional thinking and of rejecting science.

"Flew has, sadly, lost it!"[15] one critic wrote.

But Flew tenaciously defended his beliefs. "I have been denounced by [my former colleagues] for stupidity, betrayal, senility and everything you can think of, and none of them have read a word that I have ever written"[16] he reflected. What had Flew done that was so upsetting?

---

[14] N.P. Pharyngula, "Science Blogs," April 29, 2013.

[15] Ibid.

[16] Gamble, Dave (25 May 2014). "Antony Flew – did he really change his mind?" Skeptical-Science.com.

He simply changed his mind.

Once a highly influential atheist, Flew mysteriously became one of the people he had formerly mocked – a believer in God. His former colleagues and fans were shocked, appalled, and even infuriated.

Known for his intellectual honesty, his prolific writing, and his vigorous debates, this British philosopher was once admired by academics and atheists around the world.

At the age of fifteen, Flew concluded that there was no God. After studying philosophy, he became a professor at Oxford and several other universities in England. It was during this time that Flew became well known for his rigorous academic atheism.

But in 2004, in his early 80s, Flew gave a startling revelation that sent shockwaves through the philosophical and scientific communities – shockwaves that still reverberate to this day. During an interview with Dr. Gary Habermas,[17] Antony Flew revealed that he now believed in the existence of an intelligent Designer of some kind.

The *atheist* had dropped the "*a*" and was now a *theist*.

Antony Flew had changed his mind!

How did this happen? Can intelligent, well-educated people really believe in God? What actual science is involved in the notion of intelligent design? Does this belief automatically disqualify a person

---

[17] Antony Flew and Gary Habermas, "My Pilgrimage from Atheism to Theism," Philosophia Christi 6, no. 2 (2004): 197–211, https://doi.org/10.5840/pc20046224

from being a "real scientist"? What arguments or facts led Antony Flew to say that he "had to go where the evidence leads?"[18]

The question of God's existence has been hotly debated for centuries. Scholars and laymen alike have wrestled with this issue. During college, I attended several lectures in which the professors even pontificated about God's existence. Like many of us, they wrestled with how we could *know for sure* that God was *actually* there.

The atheists who castigated Flew for changing his mind claimed he had gone crazy. The majority of scholars today reject the notion of intelligent design. However, it's important to note that many of the actual tenets of atheism are quite questionable. Philosopher, mathematician, and author, David Berlinski brings this fact to light with a series of audacious, yet humorous questions and answers:[19]

- Has anyone provided proof of God's inexistence? *Not even close.*
- Has quantum cosmology explained the emergence of the Universe or why it is here? *Not even close.*
- Have the sciences explained why our Universe seems to be fine-tuned to allow for the existence of life? *Not even close.*
- Are physicists and biologists willing to believe in anything so long as it is not religious thought? *Close enough.*
- Has rationalism in moral thought provided us with an understanding of what is good, what is right, and what is moral? *Not close enough.*
- Has secularism in the terrible twentieth century been a force for good? *Not even close to being close.*
- Is there a narrow and oppressive orthodoxy of thought and opinion within the sciences? *Close enough.*

---

[18] Ibid.

[19] Berlinski, David. 2008. The Devil's delusion: atheism and its scientific pretensions. New York: Crown Forum.

- Does anything in the sciences or in their philosophy justify the claim that religious belief is irrational? *Not even ballpark.*
- Is scientific atheism a frivolous exercise in intellectual contempt? *Dead on.*

Berlinski confronts the pretentious claim of atheism's intellectual superiority, dismantling it layer by layer. He also explains the considerable mathematical challenges to contemporary evolutionary theories in his many books and debates.

But wait a minute! What about all the smart people who are atheists? Take, for example, the late Stephen Hawking, renowned astrophysicist, considered to be one of the smartest people in the world. Hawking tiptoed for years between agnosticism, atheism, and what seemed like some form of belief, before finally concluding that God didn't exist. "No one created our universe, and no one directs our fate," Hawking wrote. "This leads me to a profound realization; there is probably no heaven, and no afterlife either. We have this one life to appreciate..."[20]

One argument frequently touted in favor of atheism is that "everyone knows that most scientists are atheists." Several years ago, a friend asked me why so many smart people, like Stephen Hawking, were skeptical of God. I responded with another question. "Have you heard of Dr. John Polkinghorne, who worked alongside Dr. Hawking? He examined the same data, used the same tools, and wrote similar books on physics. But he's a committed believer in God!"

Truth be told, many intelligent and educated people believe in God. They carefully examine the data, ultimately concluding that the

---

[20] Hawking, Stephen, Eddie Redmayne, Kip S. Thorne, and Lucy Hawking. 2020. Brief Answers to the Big Questions. London, England: John Murray.

evidence affirms their belief in God (or at least doesn't contradict it). Let me share with you just a few scientists who believe that God created the universe:[21]

- Hugh Ross is an astrophysicist who has studied quasars and galaxies. According to Ross, "Discoveries in astronomy first alerted me to the existence of God, and to this day the Bible's unfathomable depths, predictive power, and remarkable applicability to life rank as major reasons for my faith." Ross directs a science apologetics organization called *Reasons to Believe*.

- Francis S. Collins is the director of the Human Genome Project. He leads a consortium of scientists to decode DNA. When asked about the conflict between faith and science, Collins said, "I don't believe there is an inherent conflict, but I believe that humans, in our imperfect nature, sometimes imagine conflicts where there are none." Collins explains his faith more fully in his 2006 bestselling book, *The Language of God: A Scientist Presents Evidence for Belief*.

- Professor Derek Barton, who won the Nobel Prize in Chemistry, wrote that, "There is no incompatibility between science and religion. Both are seeking the same truth."

- Vera Kistiakowsky, research physicist and former professor at MIT, writes, "I am satisfied with the existence of an unknowable source of divine order and purpose and do not find this in conflict with being a practicing Christian."

- Arno Penzias won the Nobel Prize in Physics for observing universal microwave background radiation. Penzias claims that "...by looking at the order in the world, we can infer purpose,

---

[21] Dr. Robert Kurland, "23 Famous Scientists Who Are Not Atheists," Magis Center, May 19, 2019, https://magiscenter.com/23-famous-scientists-who-are-not-atheists/ (Sourced here)

and from purpose, we begin to get some knowledge of the Creator, the Planner of all this."

- Sir Neville Mott, Cambridge professor who won the Nobel Prize for his work in solid-state physics, writes "...we can and must ask God which way we ought to go, what we ought to do, how we ought to behave."

- Werner Arber, Swiss microbiologist and geneticist, shared the 1978 Nobel Prize in Physiology/Medicine for discovering restriction enzymes. "I consider that life only starts at the level of a functional cell," Arber writes. "The most primitive cells may require at least several hundred specific biological macromolecules. How such complex structures may have come together, remains a mystery to me. The possibility of the existence of a Creator, of God, represents to me a satisfactory solution to this problem."

- Tyler VanderWeele, epidemiologist, biostatistician, Harvard professor, and researcher for the Human Flourishing project writes: "It's very difficult for me to look at our world and the discoveries of science and not to see a designer."

- Andrew Wyllie, former dean of pathology at the University of Cambridge, discovered the significance of natural cell death (apoptosis). Wyllie credited his Christian belief in the resurrection with helping him discover and accept that natural cell death was part of life.

- Daniel E. Hastings, a renowned physicist and MIT professor known for his contributions to space exploration, writes, "There is a God who created the universe we can actually find God here – both through his word, and also through reason applied to his creation. If I were to describe myself, I would say I'm a *reasoning* Christian."

- Ian Hutchinson, nuclear science and engineering professor at MIT, and author of *Can a Scientist Believe in Miracles*, writes: "There is a very commonplace myth that has been promoted for the last 140 years or so, which is that science and religion are inevitably at war and always have been. But that's actually a myth The people during the scientific revolution and shortly thereafter, who made science what it is Newton and Boyle and Kepler and Galileo and people like that – these people were predominantly Christians."

- Ard Louis teaches theoretical chemistry at Oxford University. "I think the more we learn about the world," says Louis, "it points *more* towards God, rather than less."

- Owen Gingerich, renowned astronomer, physicist, and professor emeritus at Harvard, wrote an outstanding book called *God's Universe*. "Just as I believe that the Book of Scripture illumines the pathway to God, so I believe that the Book of Nature suggests a God of purpose and a God of design," he wrote. "And I think my belief makes me no less a scientist."

There's not enough room in this book to list all the 21st century, award-winning scientists and researchers who are committed theists, many of them Christians. These scientists are convinced that the Universe reveals the intelligence and purpose of a Grand Designer. Contrary to popular opinion, a top-tier scientific education is no guarantee of religious disinterest, skepticism, or unbelief. So then, like David Berlinksi above, let's examine the problem of atheism.

Problem, you say?

Yes, *problem*! Atheism presents some real challenges to the rational mind.

The Problem of Atheism

Let's start with some definitions. According to the Cambridge Dictionary of American English, an atheist is *"someone who believes that God does not exist."*[22]

The word atheism consists of two Greek words, the alpha *"a"* which means without, and the word *"theos,"* which means, God. Atheism essentially means "without God."

But in my view, these standard definitions are quite problematic.

Let me explain why.

There are many reasons why a person might claim to be an atheist. Some people reject God based on the scientific theories they've been taught. Others dismiss Him after hearing skewed, unbiblical beliefs about what God is like and how he treats people. Still others turn away after painful and traumatic experiences. Many times, what people are (rightly) rejecting is a false, medieval picture of an arbitrary and unkind God.

False portrayals of God are intellectually irrational, emotionally unattractive, and psychologically damaging.

But does atheism hold up to close scrutiny? This definitive claim about the absolute absence of God constitutes a *worldview* because it informs the atheist's perspective on all of life. This worldview is often called materialism or naturalism. Some say that atheism is not a worldview, but merely a rejection of the theistic worldview.

---

[22] Paul Procter, Cambridge International Dictionary of English (Cambridge: Cambridge University Press, 1995).

I believe atheism is a worldview. Why? Because the *no God* stance is a positive and absolute proclamation that *God does not exist* and, moreover, that *we know it*. Let's examine this point further.

Imagine that two detectives are investigating a case. One detective offers a perspective on what he believes may have happened at the crime scene. The other detective rejects his colleague's theory, but provides no alternative.

Would you say the second detective is a *good investigator*?

Those who argue that atheism is merely a rejection of God, but fail to offer sound evidence that God *doesn't* exist, are actually advocating for a position more like *agnosticism*, which simply means "not knowing."

Atheism and *agnosticism* are not the same concept. The first is a positive declaration of God's absolute non-existence. The second is merely an admission of one's uncertainty. But does the committed atheist really *know* that God doesn't exist? Trying to prove an absolute negative is a very tall philosophical and intellectual task.

In one article, "Is Atheism Logical?", the author writes:

> Atheism positively affirms that there is no God. But can the atheist be confident of this claim? You see, to know that a transcendent God does not exist would require a perfect knowledge of all things (omniscience). To attain this knowledge, you would have to have simultaneous access to all parts of the Universe (omnipresence). Therefore, as an atheist, to be sure of this claim, one would have to possess Godlike characteristics. Obviously, humanity's limited nature precludes these special abilities. The

atheist's dogmatic claim is, therefore, clearly unjustifiable. The atheist is attempting to prove a universal negative. In terms of logic, this is called a logical fallacy.[23]

In other words, knowing for certain that God doesn't exist would require access to *all* knowledge *ever*. Since human beings don't have this access, they can't denounce God's existence without engaging in a logical fallacy known in philosophy as "proving a negative."[24]

The journey of science is the ever-increasing understanding of that which was not previously known. Even the most committed atheistic scientist would confess this. By claiming that God does not exist, atheism assumes exhaustive and absolute knowledge – knowledge that human beings simply don't have. Sure, a person might *suspect* that there is no God, but no one truly *knows* that there is no God.

Some atheists are honest about this proverbial fly in the ointment of atheism. A few years ago, as I traveled to a speaking appointment in England, I saw billboards and banners with an interesting, but less than compelling slogan: *"There's probably no God."*

"...Probably?"

The public campaign[25] was supported by the famous evolutionary biologist, Richard Dawkins, probably the world's most famous and outspoken atheist at the time. Although Dawkins and the other architects of the campaign were endeavoring to spread the message of atheism far and wide, their message contained a subtle

---

[23] "God vs. Atheism: Is Atheism Logical?," Christian Research Institute, March 13, 2009, https://www.equip.org/perspectives/god-vs-atheism-is-atheism-logical/

[24] T. Edward Damer, Attacking Faulty Reasoning: A Practical Guide to Fallacy-Free Arguments (Boston, MA: Wadsworth, Cengage Learning, 2013), 17.

[25] British Humanist Association, "The Bus Campaign," February 20, 2012.

yet inconvenient truth: They themselves didn't possess the *absolute knowledge* required in order to *definitively* claim that God doesn't exist. Hence, the insertion of the word "*probably.*"

We must always recognize that, in the vast realm of the unknown, there's much more to discover and learn than we've ever conceived of. God may not fit in the minds of people who'd rather not believe in Him, but there's plenty of room for Him in the unknown.

What about Agnosticism?

If atheism is illogical, is agnosticism the way forward?

Unlike atheists, agnostics are willing to admit their own uncertainty. But agnostics make some logical mistakes too.

According to philosopher and professor J. Budziszewski:

"To say that we cannot know anything about God *is to say something about God*; it is to say that if there is a God, he is unknowable. But in that case, he is not entirely unknowable, for the agnostic certainly thinks that we can know one thing about him: That nothing else can be known about him. In the end, agnosticism is an *illogical position* to hold to."[26]

Here again, the absolute position backfires. To say that we cannot know about God is, in fact, to say that we *do know* at least one thing.

But if we know one thing, why couldn't we know two, or three, or even more?

---

[26] Ron Rhodes, Answering the Objections of Atheists, Agnostics, & Skeptics (Eugene, Or.: Harvest House Publishers, 2006), 25.

When someone claims to be an agnostic, I try to politely remind them of this: When you state that one cannot know *anything* about God, you're claiming that you know *something* about God.

Interestingly, some aspects of Hindu pantheism promote similar notions about God. The thinking goes that God is so great, and so beyond comprehension, that it's impossible for any human being to truly know Him.

Once, after I spoke in India to a group of Hindu, Muslim, and Christian college students, a Hindu lady approached me and asked in an incredulous tone: "*You* know God? How can *you* say *you* know God?!"

There's no doubt that the infinite Creator is, in some ways, unfathomable to the human mind. He transcends human thought and explanation. Our brains, as complex as they are, are incapable of unraveling many of His mysteries.

That being said, agnostics and some pantheists (like the lady mentioned above) fail to ask a crucially important question:

What if this all-powerful Creator chooses to make Himself knowable and discoverable? What then?

If God is almighty, He isn't bound by the limitations we ascribe to Him. He can make choices that reflect His desires. Scripture makes it clear that God desires to be known and loved. In fact, the whole premise of the Bible is not that man reached upward *to grasp* the *infinite*, but rather that God reached down *to embrace finite humanity*. Why? Because He's a personal God who wants to be known.

The starting point of all Scripture is that life and existence is God's responsibility. In the opening words of Genesis, we find the words: "In the beginning, God created..."[27] There's no argument here regarding God's existence or creative power, but simply a declaration that He exists and *that* He creates. Why is this?

I believe it's *because God is more real and truer* than anything else in the Universe. He is the greatest and most obvious truth ever. Perhaps this is why the ancient psalmist declared:

"The fool has said, there is no God." (Psalm 14:1)

Of course, many intelligent people today deny God's existence. Believers won't convince them otherwise by insulting them. As I've already mentioned, doubts about God can be based in trauma or erroneous theology. But regardless of where doubts come from, they don't negate the fact that God is the great Truth – the very Epicenter of all reality. We will explore this idea more fully in the next chapter.

Tracing from Cause to Effect

I can't help but wonder, why are so many people adamant about God's non-existence? Why are people eager to remain ignorant or uncertain of His presence? Since scientists and philosophers claim that much knowledge is yet to be discovered, why do so many people recoil from the possibility that God is real?

In my view, many passionate unbelievers generally aren't interested in the nuanced tensions between faith and science. They haven't necessarily studied the problems of sequence and chronology in the fossil record. They haven't thought through the anthropological arguments against the evolutionary theory, or grappled with the

---

[27] Gen. 1:1

complexities of microbiology and human life. Many unbelievers aren't card-carrying members of the intellectual atheism club.

They simply choose not to believe.

But why?

Because the picture of God they've been presented with is, well, pretty *un*believable.

Who wants to believe in a medieval God who torments people forever? Who wants to believe in a God who is aloof and indifferent to the struggles of humanity? Who wants to believe in a God who predestined some to be poor, and some to be rich – ordained some people to be saved, and some to be lost? Many of these false caricatures of God arose during the Middle Ages, but crept their way into mainstream Christian thinking.

Bad religion has played an enormous role in producing many atheists and skeptics. Don't believe me? Just look at some of the movements that rose up in response to the poor theology of the Middle Ages – everything from Darwinism and Nihilism to other variations of atheistic philosophy.

And what about the injustices, both ancient and modern, committed in the name of God? Hasn't history documented the church's violence, racism, mistreatment of women, and political corruption? What about those sleazy, money-hungry televangelists who perpetually overpromise and under deliver?

All of these experiences *misrepresent* God. I myself am atheistic toward these portrayals of God. And you should be too. These portrayals depict a God that doesn't exist – a God nothing like the One I know. As I listen to atheists and agnostics, I often find myself agreeing with their objections. *I don't believe in that kind of God either! But I do believe in a different kind of God!*

I hope that my friends who have given up on God will one day discover who He truly is. In the midst of the confusion, Scripture paints a beautiful and compelling picture of a God who is good – a God worth getting to know.

THINKING ABOUT GOD'S EXISTENCE:

- What's the definition of atheism? Why is this definition problematic?

- What does agnostic mean? Why is this definition also problematic?

- How would you respond to someone who says, "What about all the scientists who are atheists?"

- What kind of God do you *not* believe in?

Chapter 4

The *Crime Scene* of God

I used to listen to audiobooks of Sherlock Holmes, the brilliant British detective who could solve almost any mystery. It's easy to become a fan of his incredible deductive reasoning. Holmes had an uncanny ability to observe a string of seemingly minor details, only to deduce thrillingly accurate conclusions from his observations.

It's hard work to be a real detective. The detective must arrive at the crime scene, observe the facts, interview witnesses, thoroughly review the evidence, formulate a hypothesis, and hopefully follow through with an accurate evaluation and judgment.

Former homicide detective and author J. Warner Wallace points out[28] that when often observing a crime scene, the investigator must determine if the death was the result of natural causes, an accident, a suicide, or a *homicide*.

---

[28] J. Warner Wallace, God's Crime Scene: A Cold-Case Detective Examines the Evidence for a Divinely Created Universe (Colorado Springs, CO: David C. Cook, 2015).

Wallace writes, "Every homicide case begins as a simple death investigation. When a dead body is discovered, detectives must investigate the evidence to determine the most reasonable explanation. Did the person die naturally? Was an accident involved? Did he or she commit suicide? Is murder a possibility? These are the four possible explanations at any death scene. Homicide detectives are primarily concerned with the last one."[29]

Three of these scenarios could occur to a person alone in a room. Only one would require the intrusion of an enemy. Wallace explains that when forming this hypothesis, the investigator must assess the evidence *in the room*. If the evidence can't be explained by remaining inside the home, an intruder — someone from outside the room — will be suspected.

The death scene would then become a *crime scene.*

Mysteries aren't always sad, of course. Sometimes we investigate situations to determine what went right instead of wrong. For example, during my time at the Christian college I attended, I often didn't know how I would pay my tuition. Multiple times, the bill was paid anonymously. The generous donors were "outside" of my awareness, but came "inside" of my problem to help. I tried to identify who these people were, but my investigations proved futile.

Perhaps the greatest of all investigations is the examination of the universe around us. As we explore our surroundings, our existence, and our world at large, something fascinating emerges – life! The presence of life is more complex to explain than a Sherlock Holmes murder mystery.

Can all that we observe in the universe be explained solely from causes found "within the room" of the natural world, or is there

---

[29] Ibid.

evidence of an Outsider? Is life caused by natural and "internal" factors or does it require an external explanation?

Is there a Divine Outsider?

As we explore the question of the Divine Outsider, I have another question for you — a math question.

Do you think that math was *discovered* or *invented*?

Did human beings imagine and create the fundamental mathematical and logical realities that we depend on today, or were they embedded in the universe before humans came on the scene? This age-old question has divided philosophers and mathematicians into various camps. Its answer profoundly impacts our understanding of the universe.

If math is discovered rather than invented, the question should arise: Why?

Whether or not we enjoy solving math problems, all of us depend on math every day. When we catch a flight, drive a car, use our phones, wear our clothes, cook our food, and enjoy our homes, we are depending on math in ways we don't even realize.

The universe we live in contains many consistent mathematical patterns — cause and effect relationships that we easily take for granted. Take for example, Fibonacci's Sequence. This numerical pattern is a series of numbers, starting with 0 and 1, in which each number (besides 0) equals the sum of the two preceding numbers.

The Fibonacci Sequence goes like this: 0, 1, 1, 2, 3, 5, 8, 13, 21, 34, 55, 89, 144, and so on...

Why does this *sequence* matter?

Surprisingly, this unique numerical pattern shows up many places in nature and human activity. It's been identified in certain flower petal arrangements, various seeds, the structure of pineapple, and the design of the bronchi of the lungs. The Fibonacci Sequence can be found in certain works of art and music. It's even used in the stock market to predict future price changes. This seemingly intelligent mathematical pattern appears in multiple environments, indicating that "math" is very present in our world – present in ways that humans couldn't have dreamed up on their own.

Knot theory, a mathematical theory that studies "closed curves in three dimensions, and their possible deformations without one part cutting through another,"[30] was first studied in the late 18th century. A hundred years later, knot theory aided our understanding of DNA and even of the structure of the Universe. The incredible accuracy with which our mathematical system models the Universe continues to amaze researchers.

Late theoretical physicist Eugene Wigner suggested that math seems "unnaturally natural." In 1960, he published a widely read and quoted article titled, *The Unreasonable Effectiveness of Mathematics in the Natural Sciences*. Dr. Wigner described how, over and over again, a mathematical equation identified in one context has later been discovered in nature or used to understand vital lessons in physics, "by showing how the Universe has always been."[31] Similarly, Galileo Galilei once said that "mathematics is the language with which God created the Universe."[32]

---

[30] "Knot Theory," in Encyclopedia Britannica, 2019, https://www.britannica.com/science/knot-theory

[31] Eugene P. Wigner, "The Unreasonable Effectiveness of Mathematics in the Natural Sciences. Richard Courant Lecture in Mathematical Sciences Delivered at New York University, May 11, 1959," Communications on Pure and Applied Mathematics 13, no. 1 (February 1960): 1–14, https://doi.org/10.1002/cpa.3160130102

[32] Margaret L. Lial, Charles D. Miller, and E. John Hornsby, Beginning Algebra: Student's Study Guide (New York, NY: Harper Collins Publishers, 1992).

A Finely Tuned Universe

Our universe exists within the context of laws and constraints that promote survival and stability. These parameters, are so precise, in some cases, that any alteration – however minor – would compromise all life entirely. That's why these parameters are sometimes called *anthropological constraints*, referring to the significant impact they have on human life. These constraints suggest that our universe has been *finely tuned*.

Here are a few examples:[33]

1. Planet earth has only one nearby star (the sun). If it had more than one, earth's orbit would be disrupted by tidal interactions. If earth had less than one nearby star (i.e. the sun was farther away) earth wouldn't be warm enough to produce or maintain life.

2. If the surface gravity of the earth was any stronger, earth's atmosphere would be filled with poisonous air (ammonia and methane). If the surface gravity was any weaker, earth's atmosphere would lose too much water.

3. If the sun was farther away from earth, the ocean would freeze. If the sun was closer to earth, the ocean would boil.

4. If earth's gravitational interaction with the moon was stronger, the ocean's tidal changes would cause destructive tsunamis. A weaker gravitational interaction would cause climate and weather instabilities.

5. If the general seismic activity of the earth was greater, large-scale and frequent earthquakes would threaten life. If

---

[33] "Reasons to Believe: Design and the Anthropic Principle," April 29, 2013.

the activity was weaker, nutrients on ocean floors wouldn't be uplifted. Ocean life and diversity would suffer, resulting in a weakened ecosystem.

6. If earth's axial tilt was greater, the earth's surface temperature would be too hot. If earth's axial tilt was less than it is, the seasons would be too extreme to maintain life.

Have you ever watched a horrifying apocalyptic movie in which the human race is threatened by an unprecedented natural disaster? A story like this could easily become true with only a slight shift in any of these "parameters." Some of the specifications above are so precise that if they were altered by only a fraction of a fraction of a fraction of a percentage, life on planet earth would be impossible.

"The cliché that 'life is balanced on a knife-edge' is a staggering understatement in this case: no knife in the universe could have an edge that fine." [34]

Although these few parameters describe the relationship of the earth to our solar system, they don't take into account the many other constants and parameters which exist for the whole universe. According to astrophysicist Hugh Ross, this broader understanding "leads safely to the conclusion that much fewer than a trillionth of a trillionth of a percent of all stars will have a planet capable of sustaining life. Considering that the Universe contains only about a trillion galaxies, each averaging a hundred billion stars, we can see that not even one planet would be expected, by natural processes alone, to possess the necessary conditions to sustain life."[35]

---

[34] P. C. W. Davies, Cosmic Jackpot: Why Our Universe Is Just Right for Life (Boston, MA: Houghton Mifflin, 2007).

[35] Ibid.

Given the extremely (like imaginably) low probability of a "life-friendly" universe creating itself, doesn't it seem reasonable to consider the possibility that an intelligent Designer has intricately "fine-tuned" these factors to accommodate human life? Doesn't a world specifically designed for human, plant, and animal life strongly suggest outside intervention? As physicist Freeman Dyson described, "this is a universe that knew we were coming."[36]

Someone wanted us to exist.

If I traveled to the moon and found a glass aquarium full of healthy fish, wouldn't it be logical for me to conclude that someone had placed the aquarium there? Given the hostile living conditions on the moon, how else would I be able to account for the presence of the fish? Earth is like that aquarium. Although surrounded by an environment hostile to life, it somehow continues to support life.

When beautiful creatures capture our attention, when we're stunned by a remarkable sunset or hold a delicately tinted flower in our hands, it's natural to wonder about the Designer behind the design. When we understand the delicate parameters of the "knife-edge" we're on, reason comes galloping in and cries: *"There must be a God."*

Even Darwin had moments like this.

George Douglas Campbell described a fascinating visit with Charles Darwin in the last year of Darwin's life:

> "In the course of that conversation I said to Mr. Darwin, with reference to some of his own remarkable works on Fertilization of Orchids, and upon The Earthworms, and various other observations he had made of the wonderful contrivances for

---

[36] Gingerich, O., & Peter, G. (2006). God's universe. Cambridge, MA: Belknap.

certain purposes of Nature – I said it was impossible to look at these without seeing that they were the effect of mind. I shall never forget Mr. Darwin's answer. He looked at me very hard, and said: "Well, that often comes with overwhelming force; but at other times,' and he shook his head vaguely, adding, 'it seems to go away.'"[37]

The Big Bang

When you think of the word chance, what comes to mind? Getting a lucky break? Winning the lottery? Webster's Dictionary defines chance as *"something that happens unpredictably without discernible intention or observable cause."*[38] In other words, chance occurs without intentional causation.

Many people believe that all of the life, beauty, order, and diversity found in our world are simply the product of an innumerable series of chances. Of course, you can believe this if you wish – the choice is up to you. But, let's be honest, this perspective requires faith (*and a lot of it*).

You've heard of the Big Bang Theory – today's most popular explanation for the origin of the earth. But have you ever considered the astronomical odds that would have been overcome in order for this to happen? What are the chances that an ancient explosion would have been big enough to expand matter throughout the entire known universe?

---

[37] Davies, P. C. W. Cosmic jackpot: Why our universe is just right for life. Boston: Houghton Mifflin, 2007

[38] Merriam-Webster, Merriam Webster's Collegiate Dictionary (Springfield, IL: Merriam-Webster, 2014).

First ingredient: A Universe

Oxford physicist Sir Roger Penrose has calculated that the odds of our Universe's low entropy condition occurring by chance alone are on the order of 10^(10^123), an inconceivably large number.[39] This low entropy state is necessary to maintain the order of our world.

Second ingredient: A Solar System

Let's suppose that the Big Bang did happen. Earth would still have needed a solar system and some kind of large star (like our sun) to sustain life. How likely is it that a solar system like ours occurred by chance, exactly in the right place? The odds of our solar system being formed instantly by the random collision of particles are about 1 in $10^{10(60)}$, an enormous number.

Third Ingredient: An Earth-Like Planet

We're encouraged to believe that planet earth also formed by chance. But according to astrophysicist Dr. Hugh Ross, the odds of the universe producing a single earth-like planet are quite slim. After considering 123 parameters, Dr. Ross calculated that the chances of a single "earth" appearing are *"less than one chance in 10 to the 139th power (ten thousand trillion trillion trillion trillion trillion trillion trillion trillion trillion trillion) exists that even one such planet would occur anywhere in the Universe."*[40]

Wow.

---

[39] Roger Penrose, The Road to Reality: A Complete Guide to the Laws of the Universe (New York, NY: Vintage Books, Cop, 2007).

[40] "The Probability of Earth," April 29, 2013.

Of course, these odds only address the most basic elements needed for life to exist. They don't take into consideration the multitude of additional physical and biological factors that make our planet a suitable and delightful home for billions of organisms, including human beings

Fourth ingredient: Building blocks for life

Now that we've examined the probability of our planet existing by chance, let's consider the probability of human life spontaneously coming into existence.

Proteins are one of the building blocks of the human body. Our bones, skin, muscles, organs, fingernails, and toenails are all composed of proteins. Scientists now estimate that the human body contains between 80,000 and 400,000 proteins.[41] These proteins perform a wide variety of life-sustaining functions. The primary job of DNA (our genes) is to make proteins.

Proteins are chains of amino acids folding into three-dimensional shapes. Different combinations of amino acids form different kinds of proteins.

In his book, *Signature in the Cell: DNA and the Evidence for Intelligent Design*, Dr. Stephen Myer explains that "the probability of finding a functional protein [in the universe] by chance alone is a trillion, trillion, trillion, trillion, trillion, trillion, trillion times smaller than the odds of finding a single specified particle among all the particles in the Universe."[42]

---

[41] Tim Schroder, "The Protein Puzzle," n.d., https://www.mpg.de/11447687/W003_Biology_medicine_054-059.pdf

[42] Stephen C. Meyer, Signature in the Cell: DNA and the Evidence for Intelligent Design (New York, NY: Harperone, 2010).

From an evolutionary perspective, all the proteins needed for human life developed gradually over vast periods of time, beginning with a much simpler life form. However, trying to evolve anything, starting with anything, that requires more than a few dozen specifically arranged amino acid residues, is statistically impossible.

We can learn another lesson from *Mycoplasma Genitalium*, a tiny bacterium that inhabits the human urinary tract. One of the most simple life forms, this bacteria requires 'only' 482 proteins to perform its functions." In order for this bacteria to have evolved, amino acids would have had to congregate in a specified sequence with peptide links. The probability of building a chain of 150 amino acids containing only peptide links is about one in 10 to the 45th power.[43] This gives us an idea of the minimal structural requirements required for even the simplest life forms.

That's impossible!

Now that we've considered the probability of our solar system, earth, and the basic building blocks of life occurring by chance, imagine combining each of these together to assess the likelihood that *all of them* could happen. The resulting probability would be so inestimable that it would be considered impossible. Statisticians, as a general rule, consider any "possibility" with less than one in 10^{50} chance of occurring to be impossible.[44]

The "Multiverse" claims of modern atheistic physicists like Lawrence M. Krauss and his book *A Universe from Nothing* are worth mentioning. The Multiverse idea is a hypothetical collection of "potentially diverse observable universes, each of which would comprise everything

---

[43] Ibid.

[44] James S. Spiegel, The Making of an Atheist: How Immorality Leads to Unbelief (Chicago, IL: Moody Publishers, 2010), 46.

that is experimentally accessible by a connected community of observers."[45] In other words, we live in a metauniverse where there are an infinite number of possibilities for anything to occur.

Outlandish and no evidence? *Yes.*

Of course, when challenged, based on this idea, that no evidence could possibly be presented that would convince Krauss of God's existence, Krauss responded:

> "That's a true statement and very convenient for atheists who don't want to be accountable to God, don't you think?... You talk about this god of love and everything else. But somehow if you don't believe in him, you don't get any of the benefits, so you have to believe. And then if you do anything wrong, you're going to be judged for it. I don't want to be judged by god; *that's the bottom line.*"[46]

And that's the bottom line. Without any real evidence, this "ace up the sleeve" is often presented as a scientific end *all* but isn't truly verifiable in any way. In short, it's not about the evidence for atheists like Krauss. It's about a desperate effort to avoid moral judgment – and that's the bottom line.

Did We Hit the Jackpot?

Imagine if you had a friend win the lottery in August, then win it again the next August, then again the following year – for

---

[45] Anthony Aguirre, "Multiverse | Definition, Types, & Facts," in Encyclopedia Britannica, December 19, 2018, https://www.britannica.com/science/multiverse

[46] Brierley Justin, "A Universe from Nothing? Lawrence Krauss & Rodney Holder," Unbelievable, June 23, 2014, https://unbelievable.podbean.com/e/a-universe-from-nothing-lawrence-krauss-rodney-holder-unbelievable-28-apr-2012/

ten years straight. How many years would pass before a federal investigation would begin?

Are we really willing to believe that our solar system, our life-sustaining planet, and the building blocks of life came together by chance? Shouldn't this extremely unlikely theory raise our suspicions, motivating us to explore alternative explanations?

According to the late Cambridge University astrophysicist Fred Hoyle, "A common-sense interpretation of the facts suggests that a super-intellect has monkeyed with physics, as well as with chemistry and biology and that there are no blind forces worth speaking about in nature. The numbers one calculates from the facts seem to be so overwhelming as to put this conclusion almost beyond question."[47]

You may have teachers, friends, or other people in your life who claim that intelligent design is an unscientific fairy tale. Chances are, these people are either unaware of, or are flatly ignoring, the statistical odds stacked against their perspective.

I'm convinced that it's much more reasonable to hypothesize that an original Source of life *outside* our physical universe brought it into existence. I believe that Source is the Creator God described in the Bible. He is the most likely explanation of our Universe, our galaxy, our solar system, our planet, and our own lives.

It seems that only Someone infinite in power — able to work outside of natural law and beyond time itself — would have been capable of creating life as we presently understand and experience it. Nothing

---

[47] Fred Hoyle, "The Universe: Past and Present Reflections," Annual Review of Astronomy and Astrophysics 20, no. 1 (September 1982): 8–12.

short of Omnipotence can explain the world in which we find ourselves.

It takes faith to believe God exists, but even more faith to believe He doesn't.

Imagine you walk outside your house to pick up the daily newspaper from your front porch. The headline warns, *"Tiger Escaped From Local Zoo!"* The news is disturbing, but you assume the tiger must be on the other side of town.

As you walk around the side of your house, you're horrified to discover your neighbor's dog lying dead, with significant puncture wounds on its neck. Startled and scared, you swiftly head down the path towards your backyard, only to discover enormous cat-prints in the mud. Suddenly, you hear a blood-curdling roar.

What would you do?

Would you say to yourself, *I haven't seen a tiger yet, so I shouldn't assume there is one?* Or would you say, *I think this cat is crouching in my backyard?* This evidenced-based approach is the same kind of thinking that motivates the intelligent design movement. By looking at the *visible* evidence that points to what is presently *invisible*, we can see the "fingerprints" of an intelligent being.

This is why the renowned academic atheist Antony Flew, when questioned about his remarkable change of mind regarding God's existence, stated that "the most impressive arguments for God's existence were those that are supported by recent scientific discoveries" and that "the argument to intelligent design is enormously stronger than it was when I first met it."[48]

---

[48] Ibid.

Flew was convinced that the universe reveals the intelligence of a grand Designer. So am I. You can be too!

The ancient psalmist David penned a wonderful song as he contemplated intelligent design.

> *When I consider Your heavens, the work of Your fingers,*
> *The moon and the stars, which You have ordained,*
> *What is man that You are mindful of him? (Psalm 8:3-4)*

As David saw the fingerprints of the Designer in the world around him, he couldn't help but wonder:

How can such an infinite and all-powerful Being find interest in a mere human being like me?

A friend of mine posted something fascinating on social media shortly after his daughter was born. As he stared into her face and saw her soft, feminine eyes curiously gazing back at him, he realized, "My child may not know I exist as her father, but her existence only proves my existence."

"Her existence proves my existence."

My friend's newborn was not yet able to comprehend the relationship she had with the man who held her close, but the fact that she was alive was irrefutable evidence that her father existed. She simply wouldn't be present in this world without her father.

Your existence proves God's existence.

Reader, you are a miracle of creation.

The many contributing factors leading up to your existence are more than a series of chemical or mechanical interactions. You matter. You are one of God's miracles.

As human beings, we find comfort in knowing that we've been on someone's mind. It feels good to get an unexpected text message from someone we haven't seen in awhile, or a call or letter from a faraway friend. We're wired to be noticed and cared for.

You are always on *God's* mind. This universe was made on purpose. It's not all just as Shakespeare penned in *Macbeth*, "sound and fury signifying nothing."[49]

The ancient prophet Jeremiah, under Divine inspiration, wrote some profoundly significant and encouraging words to God's struggling people:

> "Then the word of the Lord came to me, saying:
> Before I formed you in the womb, I *knew* you."[50]

Before you were born into this world, before your parents thought about their future children, or your grandparents imagined having grandchildren sit on their laps, you existed in the mind and heart of your Creator – the infinite God of the universe.

Your life, your heart, your dreams, and your relationships – all of these really matter to God. You are perpetually on His mind.

---

[49] William Shakespeare, Macbeth (Cambridge, UK: Cambridge University Press, 2012), Act 5.

[50] Jer. 1:5

Once upon an eternity, just once and never will it ever be again, God was all there was. Before you and me, before humanity, and before angels, there was just God.

Yet God was not alone, for God is love – an irreducible relational complexity of three who are one.[51]

Then God said, "Let's make *others* to love like we do."

And *here we are.*

Creation is dear to the heart of God. And you are a unique and *irreplaceable* part of His creation.

---

[51] Gibson, Ty. Twitter, Sept 20, 2020.

THINKING ABOUT APOLOGETICS:

- What does the "fine-tuning" of the universe refer to?

- Can you name at least one of the parameters that must exist to sustain life as we know it? How about two?

- What do you personally see in nature that points to a Designer?

- How does the idea that you are on God's mind make you feel? Do you feel that God loves you? Why or why not?

- How do you think God might answer King David's question, "What is mankind that You are mindful of them?" (Psalm 8)

Chapter 5

The Right Book for the Right Time

C.S. Lewis once said, "Thirst was made for water, and inquiry... for truth."[52]

As I mentioned in the first chapter, I often went to the Sikh temple and to Satsang spiritual meetings as a child. An astounding amount of spiritual literature was available. Sometimes I quietly perused the spiritual books, hungering for something to satisfy my soul. But I was mystified by what I read. I simply couldn't make sense of it.

On Sundays, I struggled to understand the discourses of the spiritual teachers as they expounded on various religious topics. This led me to believe I was incapable of understanding the things of God. I never dismissed the notion that a divine being was holding the universe together, *but who or what was He?*

---

[52] C.S. Lewis, The Great Divorce (London: Collins, 2012).

As the years went by, I was intrigued by the religions and mythologies of various cultures, including my own. But it wasn't until college that I finally discovered a religion that made sense to me. As I started studying the Bible, I could tell it was no ordinary book. In time, I became convinced that the text I held in my hands was unlike any other mythological, religious, or spiritual book. It was (and is) the very revelation of God.

> ***The Bible stands alone as a real book about real people who had real experiences with a very real God.***

Words of Life

Scripture is comprised of 66 individual books, written by 44 different authors, over a span of 1500 years. These authors include kings, generals, fishermen, and farmers. Every class of society is represented in the Bible.

> ***Scripture tells the story of God meeting humanity. It's an account of God working in, through, and for human beings.***

John Hope Franklin, scholar of African American history, wrote that the "historian is the conscience of the nation."[53] If this is true, the Bible is the ultimate historian for humanity, arranging before us chosen accounts of God meeting man. The lessons, experiences, failures, and triumphs of the Biblical characters are placed before us as a moral compass to help us navigate uncharted waters.

The Bible is unlike any other literary work. A growing amount of archaeological data confirms the credibility of Scripture. Top-level

---

[53] John Bracey and John Hope Franklin, "Race and History: Selected Essays, 1938-1988.," The Journal of American History 77, no. 2 (September 1990).

scholars continue to discovered evidence of the actual events and people documented in Scripture.

Archaeology and Scripture

Purdue University scholar Lawrence Mykytiuk lists over fifty individuals from the Bible that have been confirmed archaeologically. This list includes Israelite kings, Mesopotamian monarchs and lesser-known persons. Their names appear in archaeological inscriptions written during or very close to the time they were alive.[54] The intense standard used would probably have disqualified a lot of historical documents.

Professor Mykytiuk used the following criteria to verify the biblical names:

- Each biblical name must match the name on an authentic inscription, with no possibility of forgery (thus ruling out items from the antiquities market).

- The names (from the Bible and on the archaeological inscription) must match the same setting and time period.

- The title of the person and the father's name, when provided, should also match. [55]

Talk about a strict criteria! Most historical documents would fail that test. Archaeology is a science that continues to unfold. Data discovered tomorrow could rewrite yesterday's theories, which is why trained archaeologists can never speak emphatically about the non-existence of historical figures. Over and over again, the

---

[54] Lawrence Mykytiuk., "53 People in the Bible Confirmed Archaeologically," Biblical Archaeology Society, April 12, 2017,

[55] Ibid.

findings of archaeology have affirmed the stories of Scripture — not ambiguously, but forcefully.

Several years ago, I traveled to England for a speaking engagement. After landing in Manchester, I met a friendly British stranger at the airport. When he asked the reason for my trip, I told him I was there to give a series of Bible lectures. I told him about the credibility of the Bible and the innumerable evidences behind it, briefly mentioning the discovery of the mysterious Ryland's Scroll. *"You mean John Ryland?"* the man asked. *"His museum is here in Manchester."*

I was elated. Housed in glass at the Manchester Museum are the *John Ryland Papyri*. Barely three inches square, this fragment is the earliest known copy of any part of the New Testament. The papyrus is dated somewhere between 100-125 A.D. (though it may be even older). This indicates that John's gospel was circulated as far away as Egypt within 40 years of its composition.

As I saw the fragment of that scroll, my mind began racing.

John wrote Revelation on the island of Patmos around 90-95 A.D., and is believed to have died around 100-105 A.D..[56] If the *John Ryland Papyri* is as ancient as some scholars believe,[57] it's possible it may have been written while John the Apostle was still alive. The implications are astounding.

What captured my attention the most was what the papyrus says. It only contains a small portion of John 18:31-33, where Jesus stands before Pilate and is questioned by the Roman governor. The last part of the fragment is Pilate's question to Jesus:

---

[56] Pheme Perkins, Reading the New Testament: An Introduction (New York, NY: Paulist Press, 2012).

[57] Wilhelm Schubart, Papyri Graecae Berolinenses (Berlin, Germany: Marcus and Weber, 1911).

"Are you the king of the Jews?"

The oldest known New Testament document describes a weary Roman politician searching for truth, yet not quite willing to accept the Truth standing before him.

> **When I meet people who question the Bible's reliability, I ask them: By what criteria do you determine any historical record's credibility?**

Typically, ancient documents are considered to be reliable if multiple copies and corresponding historical data is available. These documents seem even more reliable if they were copied close to the time of the original writing. Believe it or not, most widely accepted historical documents, besides Scripture, struggle to meet this criteria. Take, for example:

- *Plato's Seven Tetralogies* – Seven copies remain. These copies date 1200 years after Plato's time, but no one questions the existence of Plato.[58]

- *Caesar's Gallic Wars* – Ten copies remain. These copies date 1000 years after the event, but no one questions whether the event occurred.

- *Tacitus' Writings* – Twenty copies remain from this first century Roman historian. These copies are dated 1,000 years after the fact, but still considered reliable.

The Bible, on the other hand, has an astounding number of ancient copies – 24,000 manuscripts for the New Testament alone. Many of

---

[58] Norman L. Geisler, Christian Apologetics (Grand Rapids, MI: Baker Book House, 2013), 307.

these manuscripts date back to only 50-100 years from the events they describe.[59] No other historical book can claim that kind of evidentiary basis — not even close. In the words of British academic F.F. Bruce, "If the New Testament were a collection of secular writings, their authenticity would generally be regarded as beyond all doubt."[60]

Who Compiled the Bible?

Skeptics sometimes denounce the Bible as nothing more than a compilation of writings chosen by church leaders who wanted religious and political control.

It's true that the Dark Ages and the Middle Ages were a tragic example of what happens when state and church combine. But does that prove that the Bible was crafted with a diabolical agenda in mind?

Not at all.

The English word "canon" comes from the Greek word *kanon* (κανών), which means "rule" or "measuring stick." Long ago, Christians began to use this term to refer to Scripture. It was used to describe which books and letters were included in the Bible, as opposed to the writings that were left out. The church didn't "officially" finalize the canon until the fifth century A.D., although compilations of inspired writings had been shared before that time.

Some people have argued that the Bible can't really be from God if human beings decided which writings it would include. But a detailed

---

[59] Ibid.

[60] F. F. Bruce, The New Testament Documents: Are They Reliable?. (Grand Rapids, MI: Eerdmans, 1974), 19.

process was in place to ensure that Scripture only contained inspired writings. Texts were assessed for dating, confirmation by Christ or the apostles, harmony with previously established holy writings, etc.

In the words of one scholar:

> "The recognition of the books of the New Testament as scriptural was overwhelmingly a natural process, not a matter of ecclesiastical regulation. The core of the New Testament *was accepted so early* that subsequent rulings do no more than recognize the obvious." [61]

The majority of text researchers agree with this perspective.

New Testament writers affirmed that Scripture already existed (long before the finalization of the canon). The apostle Peter referred to Paul's writings as Scripture in 2 Peter 3:16. The early church frequently copied and used these Scriptures. One researcher has noted that if every Bible were destroyed, we could reconstruct several portions of the New Testament using only what early church fathers had written. [62]

Scripture did not *become* inspired when the church finalized the canon. The formation of the canon was simply a recognition of its inspiration. The apostle Paul wrote that "All Scripture is given by inspiration of God.[63]" We can trust the divine origin and inspiration of Scripture.

---

[61] John Barton, How the Bible came to be (Louisville, KY: Westminster John Knox press, 1998), 85.

[62] Robert Jenkins, The Reasonableness and Certainty of the Christian Religion, 2nd ed. (London: W.B. for Richard Sare, 1708), 131.

[63] 2 Tim. 3:16

The Bible and India

India is comprised of several states, including Punjab, Tamil Nadu, Rajasthan, etc. The state of Kerala has a higher percentage of Christians than any other state in India. Kerala also happens to be *the most literate state* in India. Is there a correlation? Absolutely.

The relationship between reading God's Word and advancing in education is undeniable. In Kerala, India's most literate state, the word for school is *Pallikudam*, which means "[the building] next to the church."[64] The God who designed our minds knows how to strengthen them through His word.

For many centuries, India's lack of a mother language and the presence of multiple dialects created scores of problems. A peasant might have to travel north to go to court, only to be robbed of justice because he couldn't understand the particular dialect spoken there. In the nineteenth century, India didn't even have one scholar who could read a single sentence inscribed on the ancient King Ashoka's pillars, which are dispersed throughout India. Ashoka was a Buddhist king who attempted to unify India.

Thanks to Bible translators and missionaries in the late nineteenth century, a few Indian dialects were turned into a written language – Hindi – which became a common unifier of the people. Bible translators also helped develop several of India's other modern literary languages:

> One Indian scholar writes, "Bible translators and missionaries did not merely give me my mother tongue, Hindi. *Every living literary*

---

[64] Vishal Mangalwadi, The Book That Changed Your World: How the Bible Created the Soul of Western Civilization (Nashville, TN, 2011), 194.

language in India is a testimony to their labor. In 2005, a Malyalee scholar from Mumbai, Dr. Babu Verghese, submitted a seven-hundred-page doctoral thesis to the University of Nagpur. It demonstrated that Bible translators, using the dialects of mostly illiterate Indians, created seventy-three modern literary languages. These include the national languages of India (Hindi), Pakistan (Urdu), and Bangladesh (Bengali). Five Brahmin scholars examined Dr. Verghese's thesis and awarded him a Ph.D. in 2008."[65]

Many Indians are unaware that Bible translators helped forge India's mother tongue, Hindi, as the universal language of the land, and helped promote literacy throughout the country. The Bible was responsible for changing the cultural, social, and educational landscape of the Far East.

The Good, the Bad, and the Ugly

When you examine the spiritual literature of other faiths, you will rarely (if ever) find a record of the mistakes and sins of its heroes and protagonists. Scripture is different. The Bible contains detailed descriptions of the weaknesses of God's people. This is significant from an apologetic perspective. In the words of one commentator:

> "Inspiration faithfully records the faults of good men, those who were distinguished by the favor of God; indeed, *their faults are more fully presented than their virtues*. This has been a subject of wonder to many and has given the infidel occasion to scoff at the Bible."[66]

---

[65] Ibid.

[66] Ellen G. White, The Story of Patriarchs and Prophets: As Illustrated in the Lives of Holy Men of Old (Mountain View, CA: Pacific Press Pub. Assoc., 1958).

But in fact, this pattern is one of the strongest evidences of the truth of Scripture. Facts are not glossed over nor the sins of main characters suppressed.

> "Men whom God favored, and to whom He entrusted great responsibilities, were sometimes *overcome* by temptation and committed sin, even as we at the present day strive, waver, and frequently fall into error. Their lives, with all their faults and follies, are open before us, both for our encouragement and warning. If they had been represented as without fault, we, with our sinful nature, might despair at our own mistakes and failures. But seeing where others *struggled* through discouragements like our own, where they fell under temptations as we have done, and *yet took heart again* and conquered through the grace of God, we are encouraged in our striving after righteousness. As they, though sometimes beaten back, recovered their ground and were blessed of God, so we too may be overcomers in the strength of Jesus."[67]

One of the most significant evidences of the credibility of the Bible is its honest description of human beings.

In the Scriptures, we find God meeting people right where they are, not where they should be. Nothing is hidden or glossed over in the stories. Even the best human characters wrestled with their selfishness. This demonstrates how God works with broken and sinful human beings today.

How does the honesty of the Bible enhance its credibility? The fact that Scripture paints an accurate picture of humanity's condition makes it more likely that it will tell the truth about God too.

---

[67] Ibid.

What Scripture says about humanity is just as true as what it says about God.

I remember sitting in a philosophy class, listening to my professor describe human history and social evolution. He shared his belief that humanity had evolved and reached greater enlightenment because of philosophy. I thought about this for a moment, then raised my hand:

> *"But hasn't humanity been struggling with the same problems since day one? I asked. We're still plagued by murder, war, abuse, rape, and suffering. If philosophy had improved the human condition, wouldn't this have changed?"*

Suffice it to say, he didn't have an answer.

Humanity wrestles with selfishness – the root of all sin. The fruit of selfishness is greed, anger, lust, violence, destruction, and evil. Scripture clearly reveals humanity's condition and points to its only hope.

Scripture Protects

Imagine you're walking down a dark alley at night. The blinking neon lights of motels and shops flicker on the street. As you hurriedly make your way through the sketchy alley, you suddenly notice several large figures *walking your way*. Their hands are out as they move towards you.

How do you react? Better yet, how do you feel?

Let's replay the situation, but this time with some new details. Imagine you're walking down a dark alley at night. The blinking neon lights of motels and shops flicker on the street. As you hurriedly make your way through the sketchy alley, you suddenly notice several large figures *walking your way*. Their hands are out and holding Bibles.

Did you say ... Bibles?

Didn't expect that, right?

But if we had to choose one scenario over the other, most of us (believers or not) would gladly pick the second situation over the first. Why? It's generally known that those who read the Bible experience a transformation. Whether its skeptics will admit it or not, the Bible changes people.

The Bible has transformed individuals of every stripe. From all cultures and backgrounds, those who accept the principles of God's Word undergo change. Millions of Christians can testify to the fact that the goodness of God, revealed in Scripture, has produced new life in them.

This book changes hearts. Scripture has turned many people from violence to gentleness, from restlessness to peace, and from aimlessness to purpose. When people go through the Word, the Word goes through them.

It's true that many professed believers have failed to live up to the loving principles of Scripture. It would be naive (and false) to claim that every believer is a shining example of morality and kindness. God and His word have been misrepresented far too many times. At the same time, we should acknowledge that the stories and lessons of Scripture have changed many hearts for the better. The words of Jesus have motivated countless generous actions and prevented many unkind deeds. Even an honest atheist would admit that. He or she may dispute the mechanism by which this occurs, but would likely not deny the apparent effect.

God is Love

The Bible presents to us the ground zero reality of God. The apostle John wrote that: *"God is love."*[68] From this essential truth, we begin to understand the Creator of all life.

"God is love."

All the documented providences of God are to be understood through the grand attribute of love. All the doctrines of God find their DNA in this truth. Through this lens we see the shape of God's character. His blessings, his commandments, and His wisdom all flow from a heart of love.

The most accurate picture of God is found in Christ. The disciples saw Love manifested before them in the person of Jesus. His actions, His obedience, His care, His wisdom, His service, and His sacrifice all testify to what Love looks like.

Once the disciples saw Jesus, they couldn't unsee Him in the Scriptures. From the first promise of redemption given to Adam and Eve, to the warnings and predictions of the minor prophets, the disciples saw God's love on display. Jesus said: *"You search the Scriptures ... these are they which testify of Me"* (John 5:39). The Scriptures contain the greatest record of Jesus. Through Jesus, we see who God truly is.

Not only is Scripture a record of God's interactions throughout human history. It's also a channel through which we can hear His voice today. The Bible is a love letter from the heart of God to the soul of broken humanity.

---

[68] 1 Jn. 4:17

Words of Wisdom

Renowned biologist Edward O. Wilson once stated, *"We are drowning in information, while starving for wisdom."*[69]

He was right.

Today, we have endless information at our fingerprints. With a few keystrokes, we can learn about history, technology, public health, and foreign news. YouTube can teach us how to do just about anything. Our social media feeds are cluttered with articles on everything from politics to pandemics to romance. Books can be skimmed on a phone or other device. Foreign literature can be quickly translated. We're constantly barraged with endless information.

Yet, people are dying for wisdom.

- We can learn to build houses, but not homes.
- We can be entertained by funny videos, but drown in sadness.
- We can read self-help books, but question why our hearts are still broken.
- We can order anything we want at the click of a button, but feel emptier than we did before.
- We can get thousands of followers and likes on social media, but still experience great loneliness.

We need wisdom from One who understands human existence, human relationships, and the human heart. We need wisdom from One who gives satisfaction and contentment. We need the wisdom that will make us truly successful in this life.

---

[69] Edward O. Wilson, Consilience: The Unity of Knowledge (New York, NY: Knopf, 1998), 294.

Wisdom is *found* in the Word of God.

The book of Proverbs has excellent counsel for us today:

> Hear instruction and be wise,
> And do not disdain it.
> Blessed is the man/woman who listens
> Watching daily at my gates,
> Waiting at the posts of my doors.
> For whoever finds me finds life,
> And obtains favor from the Lord. [70]

Several years ago, I made the decision that I would spend time in the Bible every day. When I wake up, I pray and then read. Of all my habits, this one has shaped my life, my career, my relationships, my goals, and my growth more than anything else. Not only does the Word of God give wisdom for the past and the future, but for each and every day. Through the promises of the Bible, I find courage and strength for every trial and need I face.

As human beings, we have the privilege of communing with our Maker – the source of all wisdom, blessing, comfort, and hope. God has given us Scripture as a special guide for our lives.

So why do I believe in the Bible?

Because it's historically documented, it accurately portrays the condition of human race, changes the lives of those who read it, and reveals God's infinite love for you and me.

I feel privileged to spend time in Scripture every day. It's the word of life for my soul. It can be for you too.

---

[70] Prov. 8:33-35

THINKING ABOUT SCRIPTURE:

- What do you think is the most convincing argument for the Bible's credibility?

- How do we know that the Biblical canon is actually inspired?

- What are some reasons to believe a historical document is credible?

- How did the Bible transform India?

- What does the Bible not hide? What does this teach us about the way God relates to us?

Chapter 6

God at War:
The Problem of Evil

This next story may sound unbelievable but it did actually occur. I read about this account in different books and articles and it is widely documented.

On the evening of April 26, 2006, several students and staff from Taylor University were traveling back to campus when their van was struck head on by another vehicle. Tragically, five students died in the accident.

The Van Ryn family discovered that their daughter, Laura, was in a critical coma after surviving the crash. Day after day, they stayed by the bedside of their unconscious daughter. Laura's head injuries were so severe that, for five weeks, she was almost completely covered in bandages. Life support machines kept her alive, but the outlook seemed grim.[71]

---

[71] Mike Celizic, "Families Speak about Switched Identity Ordeal," MSNBC, March 27, 2008, https://www.today.com/news/families-speak-about-switched-identity-ordeal-1C9015997

As time went on, the young woman slowly began improving. Her parents were overjoyed with her progress. But as family members tried to communicate with her, she kept shaking her head. "I'm not Laura," she repeated. "I'm Whitney." There had been a Whitney on the trip, but she had been pronounced dead after the accident. Whitney's grieving family had already had a funeral and buried her.

What happened?

After examining dental records, the medical staff realized there had been a big mistake. Someone at the crash scene had mistakenly identified the survivor as Laura rather than Whitney. In actuality, Laura Van Ryn had died in the accident. The woman in the hospital was Whitney Cerak. DNA testing confirmed that the buried body was that of Laura Van Ryn.

A family that thought their daughter was...dead found out she was actually alive, while another family that had rejoiced in their daughter's life...discovered she had died at the crash scene weeks before.[72] Can you imagine the shock, the joy, the tears, the pain, the anger, and the confusion?

The Problem of Pain

In one of my graduate religion classes, we examined a book by Princeton Professor Stephen Prothero, who compares and contrasts various world religions. After pointing out their many differences, Prothero describes what he believes ultimately unites all religions:

---

[72] Theodore Kim, "Case of Mistaken Identity Stuns Families," USA Today, June 1, 2006, https://usatoday30.usatoday.com/news/nation/2006-05-31-indiana-mistaken-identity_x.htm

"What the world's religions share is not so much a finish line as a starting point. And where they begin is with this simple observation: Something is wrong with the world." [73]

Throughout the course of human history, people in every culture and nation have pondered this universal problem. The great truth of God's power and goodness seems undeniable, but so does the reality of suffering and death. This creates a seemingly incomprehensible dilemma.

Something is *seriously wrong* with this world.
But how do atheists and skeptics understand and explain the problem of evil and suffering?

If there is no God, there is:

- no real explanation for suffering
- no grand purpose or hope to cling to
- no divine being working to bring good out of evil
- no making of things right one day
- no justice

Nothing.

For atheists and agnostics, the world is filled with a blind, cruel, indiscriminate, and unexplainable injustice. They see the effects of sin and suffering, but can't address the true causes. They observe the "what" but cannot explain the "why."

---

[73] Stephen R. Prothero, God Is Not One: The Eight Rival Religions That Run the World, and Why Their Differences Matter (Collingwood, Vic.: Black Inc., 2011).

But the question of suffering demands to be *addressed*.

The person open to theism can ask: "*With all the beauty, art, love, and other evidences of God's goodness in our world, how can we make sense of tragedy, evil, and suffering?*

Apologists love to defend the evidence for intelligent design found in nature. This is important, but the remarkable order and beauty in our world shouldn't lead us to overlook the presence of chaos and suffering. Tremendous tension exists between goodness and evil in our world. This tension must be thoroughly analyzed and discussed. In fact, this is the question Christian apologists wrestle with more than any other:

How can God be a God of love if He allows so much evil and suffering?

Theodicy of Love

Theodicy is a word coined in the seventeenth century by Gottfried Wilhelm Leibniz,[74] one of the great intellectuals of the Enlightenment. It's an academic term used to describe attempts to reconcile God's goodness with the reality of evil in the world.

Why do we struggle with theodicy? Because we know that something is terribly wrong. In the words of philosopher Peter Kreeft:

> "The problem of evil is the most serious problem in the world. More people have abandoned their faith because of the problem of evil than for any other reason. It is certainly the greatest test of faith, the greatest temptation to unbelief. And it's not just an intellectual objection. We feel it. We live it. The problem can be

---

[74] Michael J. Murray, "The Problem of Evil in Early Modern Philosophy," Leibniz Society Review 12 (2002): 103–6, https://doi.org/10.5840/leibniz20021211

stated very simply: If God is so good, why is His world so bad? Why do bad things happen to good people?"[75]

Bad news stalks us every day. Accounts of sickness, death, pandemics, mental illness, corruption, and crime are all part of the daily makeup of our lives. With the inestimable tragedies and injustices of last year (or last week) alone, how does a believer defend the idea of an all-powerful, omnibenevolent Being?

Charles Darwin, the founder of the evolutionary theory, wrote a telling letter to his friend about the tension between faith and suffering:

> "With respect to the theological view of the question. This is always painful to me. I am bewildered. I had no intention to write atheistically. But I own that I cannot see as plainly as others do, and as I should wish to do, evidence of design and beneficence on all sides of us. *There seems to me too much misery in the world.* I cannot persuade myself that a beneficent and omnipotent God would have designedly created the [wasps] with the express intention of their [larva] feeding within the living bodies of Caterpillars, or that a cat should play with mice."[76]

This vulnerable moment and others like it, seem to hint that Darwin's research and theories were motivated by theological misgivings, not just biological curiosity. Darwin, like many others, saw violence in nature and all around him. He couldn't help but wonder why.

---

[75] Peter Kreeft, "The Problem of Evil," www.peterkreeft.com, October 27, 2016, https://www.peterkreeft.com/topics/evil.htm

[76] Charles Darwin and Francis Darwin, Charles Darwin: His Life Told in an Autobiographical Chapter, and in a Selected Series of His Published Letters (London: John Murray, 1908).

For the believer willing to wrestle and study, the answers can be found in Scripture.

When you open the Bible to Genesis 1:1, you'll read, *"In the beginning, God created the heavens and the earth."*

Here, we're introduced to a perfect God, who created a perfect world, for a perfect people, who lived in a perfect environment, in perfect health, enjoying perfect relationship with their Creator and one another. The origin of our world is Eden. Its vivid description reminds us of happiness, growth, flourishing, and love. The word *Eden* actually means pleasure. Read the first two chapters of Genesis, and you'll discover human life as God originally intended.

Now close your Bible. What do you see?

You see violence, mayhem, suffering, poverty, isolation, hunger, sickness, pain, sorrow, and death. Like a montage of horrific movie scenes, images of bombs, chaos, war, sickness, conflict, grief, and suffering can fill your mind. This is life for so many people today. Now open your Bible again. *What's the first question on your mind?*

I believe we're *supposed* to ask this particular question...

If you're still unclear about the question, imagine this scene: One day you leave your house tidy and spotless. Your clothes are freshly washed and carefully folded. Your dishes are washed and drying on the rack. The living room is freshly vacuumed, with every couch pillow in its proper place. Feeling satisfied with your work, you leave home to buy some groceries. But when you return, something has *happened*.

After unlocking the door, you find the living room in disarray. The kitchen sink is full of dirty dishes. Clothes are scattered all over your bedroom floor. Windows are broken, and several valuables are missing. *What would be your most obvious question?* (Drum roll...here we go!)

"What happened here?" ... *What happened?*

You would want to know what happened to your home and your belongings. How did it happen? Who caused it to happen? It's only natural that you would want to understand.

God wants to provide us with an understanding of theodicy. He doesn't want us to suppress our difficult questions, putting our brains on the shelf. On the contrary, He wants us to notice the stark contrast between His original design in Eden and our present reality of suffering. *God wants us to ask why.*

If this planet looks like a war zone, that's because it is one.

The tension we feel in our hearts between what once was and now is, is meant to alert us to the fact that something has gone wrong. Every human being feels this at times. When our hearts boil at injustice, or break in grief, we intrinsically know that *it shouldn't be this way!*

An Enemy Has Done This

If God is good, why is the world bad? This dilemma may be easier to solve if we slightly reword the question: If God is good, *how* did this world *become bad?*

How...?

Jesus told a parable in Matthew 13 about a man sowing good seed. Later that night, an adversary planted bad seeds in the man's field to destroy his good crop. Soon, weeds started appearing along with the crop. Jesus described how bewildered the man's servants were to see so many weeds:

> *"The landowner's servants came to him and said, 'Master, didn't you sow good seed in your field? Then where did the weeds come from?'"*[77]

The Master's response made it clear where the blame belonged. *"An enemy has done this..."* he said.

Jesus explained that this parable represented the good world God had created, and the enemy's attempts to damage that world.

Jesus wasted no time identifying the cause of the world's suffering.

He unabashedly pointed out that an antagonistic force was seeking to undermine all that is good in the Universe. The Scriptures identify this being as Lucifer, Satan, the fallen one, etc.

Of course, this leads us to another important question.

If God is good, why did He create a devil?

The short answer is that He didn't.

The Genesis account points out that God created only "good." Other passages in Scripture tell the story of a beautiful being named Lucifer making selfish decisions, falling from heaven's graces, and thus becoming the devil.

But if God is good, why did He allow this angel to turn into a devil? Better yet, why does He allow human beings to commit evil? Why not immediately stop all evil on the planet?

---

[77] Matt. 13:27

Why doesn't the most powerful Being in the Universe press the magic red button to end all evil, suffering, and death in the world? The answer is simple. It's because *God is love* that He doesn't force the will (nor remove the effects of the will) of any of His created beings.

Love and Freedom

Love is the defining essence of who God is. This attribute is more central to His character than power or control. C.S. Lewis, the famous English writer, described the connection between love and freedom:

> "God created things which had free will. That means creatures which can go wrong or right. Some people think they can imagine a creature which was free but had no possibility of going wrong, but I can't. *If a thing is free to be good it's also free to be bad.* And free will is what has made evil possible. Why, then, did God give them free will? Because free will, though it makes evil possible, is also the only thing that makes possible any love or goodness or joy worth having."[78]

If God prevented His creatures from ever committing unloving acts, programming us instead to only do loving things, would our love be genuine? Would we really have a choice? No.

Our ability to choose sets us apart from the inanimate things of this world. The capacity to make moral decisions based on principles, not circumstances, sets us even further apart from animals. Because God is love, He lets us choose. God created us with the capacity to love and be loved. But He doesn't force us to love Him or one another. Why? Because the very second something other than voluntary choice is introduced, love *ceases* to be love.

---

[78] C.S. Lewis, Mere Christianity (New York, NY: Simon & Schuster, 1996), 52–53.

Think about it. God set out to create the best possible world – a world in which love is voluntarily chosen and freely given. But in order to create this type of world, He had to give His creatures the power of choice.

God was in a pickle.

If He gave His creatures free will, they might make the wrong choices. But if He didn't, they wouldn't be free. Without freedom, love can't exist. To respond in love requires choice.

Fully aware of the risks and benefits, God chose to make us free.

Was this choice really worth the risk? Lewis believes so:

"...If God thinks this state of war in the Universe a price worth paying for free will – that is, for making a live world in which creatures can do real good or harm and something of real importance can happen, instead of a toy world which only moves when He pulls the strings – then we may take it is worth paying."[79]

Why did He create knowing this would happen?

In God's experience with Lucifer, his betrayer in heaven and Judas, his betrayer on earth, His M.O. was to give the most advantages, most incentives, and most potential to be *saved* rather than to be lost and destroyed. Why would He, when He knew they would eventually reject Him?

There are several insights to this; here's one: God operates with every being with the greatest right to life rather than death. Being the Life-giver, He creates with the intention of life and happiness for His creatures. But in order to truly accomplish this, His love-based

---
[79] Ibid

operational principles take precedence over His foreknowledge of time. These dynamics are built on maximum liberty and motivated by unselfish love. God values choice and in spite of what is known about the future, often chooses to operate in enough of the present tense in order to provide the most salvific freedom possible to the individual, which would require...*not* always revealing details about the future. God knew what would happen to Solomon, Samson, and Saul but gave them the most incentives, most benefits, most hope to do what is right. He did not always interfere to stop their decision-making; anything else would have diminished their liberty in some degree. And if God only acts based upon what He knows of the future, present freedoms would be mitigated in some sense. Simply put: *Love tries* regardless of what *Love knows*.

God presently deals with men by not what He knows, but on who He is...And that is Love.

Of course, God isn't standing idly by, watching the world suffer without trying to help. He's actively working to bring sin and suffering to an end. Only loving choices will be made in heaven. We will still have our power of choice, but every person will be fully convinced that God is good and that His principles are worth following. The Judgment will show the lengths and depths God went to in attempting to save His creations.

Dinner and a Dilemma

Several years ago, a friend and I shared an incredible Indian meal of garlic naan and paneer. As we ate together, my friend shared his goal of pursuing a philosophy degree. He also shared that he was an atheist. Naturally, I asked why he took that position:

> "Because of all the evil in the world," he said. "Why doesn't God stop it? He must not exist or must not care."

"If you were God, how would you stop the evil in the world?" I asked.

He looked down at his food for a while, then solemnly admitted, *"I'm not sure."*

The reason my friend answered this way is because he understood, in some sense, the big dilemma:

> ***How can you possibly stop all the evil in the world when the seeds of potential evil lie in the heart of human beings?***

If God took away your ability to make bad decisions, you would lose your freedom. If God were to reprogram your brain, you would be like a mindless robot. If God did anything to forcibly alter your choices, your volition, or your freedom, you would become a *what* rather than a *who*.

God didn't create the devil. He created Lucifer, an angel of light who chose to become a devil. God didn't create evil and suffering. He created angels and human beings who were perfectly free to choose love, but instead chose selfishness. While God establishes the *facts* of freedom, we commit the *acts* of freedom.

A Cosmic Controversy

Even before I became a Christian, I contemplated artists' depictions of God warring against Satan (Revelation 12:7) in the cosmic conflict between good and evil.

Have you ever wondered why the Almighty God of heaven and earth — the God with infinite power at His command — doesn't just destroy the Devil?

Apologist, professor, and writer Sean McDowell has asked this same question: *"Have you ever wondered how God and Satan could be engaged in a genuine cosmic struggle? Since God is all-powerful, and Satan is a limited being, how could they be in any genuine conflict at all?*"[80]

To solve this dilemma, some have proposed the notion of cosmic dualism, the idea that God and Satan are equally powerful beings vying for the rulership of creation. But Scripture utterly rejects this idea through its claims of God's omnipotence. God has the power to wipe out Satan and someday He will (see Revelation 20:7-10).

This isn't your typical power struggle. Something else is going on.

The conflict between God and Satan isn't about force against force, like a typical wrestling match. Something infinitely more important than ego is at stake. What is it?

Theologian John Peckham writes, "I argue that God's love (properly understood) is at the *center* of a cosmic dispute and that God's commitment to love provides a morally sufficient reason for God's allowance of evil."

Peckham goes on to explain that in the face of this evil, God *does* work to prevent and relieve suffering, but that He must operate within the "rules of engagement," which honor free will.

God's love is at the center of the conflict.

This controversy is a war of ideas. This battle is essentially *epistemic*.

Epistemology is a branch of philosophy that has to do with knowledge, belief, and truth.[81] The battle is *epistemic* because it has to do with *what we believe.*

---

[80] Sean McDowell, "How Can God and Satan Be in a Cosmic Struggle?," Sean McDowell, n.d., https://seanmcdowell.org/blog/how-can-god-and-satan-be-in-a-cosmic-struggle

How do we know this? Scripture mentions very little of Satan's physical power, detailing instead his power to twist words and ideas for his own gain. Satan is referenced as the:

- Accuser of the brethren (Revelation 12:10)
- Father of lies (John 8:44)
- Liar (John 8:44)
- Deceiver (Revelation 12:9)
- Blinder of the many minds (2 Corinthians 4:4)
- Tempter (Matthew 4:3)
- Spirit that works in the children of disobedience (Ephesians 2:2)

Peckham describes the devil's deceptive work:

"From Genesis to Revelation, questions regarding God's character and government are raised in heaven and on earth. Since the enemy's slanderous allegations are epistemic in nature, they cannot be effectively answered by any *display of power*, however great. Indeed, no amount of power exercised by a king would prove to his subject that he is not unjust. No show of executive power could clear the name of a president accused of corruption. A conflict over character cannot be settled by sheer power but requires demonstration."[82]

An enemy trafficking lies about God's character and law cannot be overcome by force.

Imagine that an employee from an investment firm contacts the media, claiming there is corruption and widespread fraud in his workplace. Soon, a juicy story appears on the front cover of the

---

[81] Matthias Steup, The Stanford Encyclopedia of Philosophy: Epistemology, ed. Edward N. Zalta, Spring 2014, 2005.

[82] Ibid.

newspaper. Key investors angrily start pulling their money out of the firm.

Let's assume the employee's claims are false. What should the firm do to clear their name?

One terrible option would be to make the man disappear or hold him captive somewhere. That would end his false claims once and for all!

Or would it? Actually, that would make the false claims seem even more credible to the public.

The only responsible option would be to truthfully address the allegations – committing to an extensive audit to prove the integrity of the firm. Power and force cannot overcome lies – especially lies about someone's character. Lies can only be overcome with truth.

Why doesn't God end the problem of evil with force? This is a shortsighted question. Any attempt to prematurely end the struggle with Divine force, may in fact prolong – and even fuel it.

> ***God can't eradicate evil permanently if He deals with it prematurely.***

God's Two Objectives

In his battle with evil, God has two objectives: the eternal security of the universe and the preservation of voluntary love (freedom).

God is committed to permanently eradicating sin and suffering from the universe. This task is more daunting than we realize. It must be done through the full display of love and the complete exposure of selfishness. The character of God and the character of Satan, fully manifested before the universe, will bring an end to the controversy.

Our world is a theater in which the principles of good and evil are playing out, not for amusement, but for the sake of truth. God is allowing everything in this world that runs counter to love to ripen fully. He must allow sin to be exposed for what it is. This process is as painful to Him as it is to us.

The fruit of evil must reach a kind of *conclusive ripening* that can be undeniably seen and understood. In the parable of the wheat and the tares, the owner of the field allows time for the good crop and the evil crop to grow, so they can be undoubtedly identified.

Free moral beings need to see, once and for all, how damaging sin is, how good God is, and how generous His principles are. This process is necessary in order to ensure that sin and suffering will not rise again. The matter must be settled in the minds and hearts of all who will live for eternity with Christ.

Finding Answers at the Cross

The cross of Calvary is the epicenter of God's solution to the problem of evil. At the cross, the true colors of both Christ and Satan are revealed. Love is contrasted with evil; righteousness with rebellion. The cross speaks down through the ages, asking us today: "Which side of this conflict do you want to be on? Do you want a leader who rules by unselfish love, or by cruel and tyrannical force? An awareness of Christ's infinite sacrifice can change our hearts – motivating us to love while still preserving our freedom of choice. God's grace is sufficient to wash our sins but also to cleanse us from unrighteousness.

The cross reveals once and for all that God does not stand aloof from human suffering. Through His sacrifice, He actively works to reverse the curse of sin.

In the words of one philosopher, "The best answer to the problem of evil is not one so much found on paper but on wood." [83]

On Calvary, the sins of the world came crashing down on Christ. The Innocent suffered the death of the guilty. All the weapons of hell were aimed at Jesus. Satan caused the Son of God as much pain as he possibly could. He tried to prove love does not exist.

Yet Jesus' infinite love proved that Satan's arguments were *false* and *causeless*. Through Christ's merciful sacrifice, the universe beheld the truth about God. Satan was exposed as a deceptive tyrant. *Love conquered.*

Jesus understood what Calvary would accomplish. Speaking of the cross, he said:

> "Now is the judgment of this world; now the ruler of this world will be cast out. And I, if I am lifted up from the earth, will draw all peoples to Myself."[84]

Satan's credibility was shattered at the cross. Today, he still tempts people to distrust God's goodness and to make selfish choices, but he knows his time is short. Those who behold Christ's love on the cross are drawn towards the Truth and away from the lies.

The Story of Job

The book of Job gives a behind-the-scenes look at the war between good and evil.

The first chapter of Job shows a man who is blessed in every conceivable way – financially, relationally, spiritually, etc. *What more can you ask for?*

---

[83] Quote attributed to Peter Kreeft (no literary source)

[84] John 12:31-32

As the curtains roll back, the text describes a gathering in heaven. Satan shows up uninvited to make a public attack on God's character. He claims that Job doesn't truly love God. "You have blessed the work of his hands, and his possessions have increased in the land," Satan says. "But now, stretch out Your hand and touch all that he has, and he will surely curse You to Your face!"[85]

Satan's ultimate claim here is that God is not worth loving. Human beings are not capable of loving Him but are only tricked into thinking they love Him when they receive His blessings. Satan is questioning the existence of love between God and human beings.

Satan questions the existence of love.

In order to refute the false claims, God gives Satan permission to remove Job's blessings. Job's life soon becomes the epicenter of the divine conflict. He loses everything – his riches, his children, his reputation, and his health. His friends blame him for his misfortune. His heartbroken wife encourages him to "curse God and die!"[86] Shaken to the core, Job continues to love God, "Though He slay me, yet will I trust Him," he says.[87]

God Knows Your Story

Like Job, each one of us struggles to find hope and meaning in the midst of our suffering.

Job's friends assumed their advice would be helpful. They were wrong. What did Job really need? Not just answers, but an audience with God. The situation didn't improve until Job had an open, honest conversation with God. This time of connection finally brought him the healing and hope he needed.

---

[85] Job 1:10-11

While it's true that we need a philosophical framework to understand suffering, in times of crisis, what we most need is the embrace of God.

Job needed more than answers; he needed an audience with God.

People who are suffering need to know that someone understands their pain. That's why Job said:

> "Oh, that my words were written! Oh, that they were inscribed in a book!" (Job 19:23)

Job wanted his story to matter to someone else. He had no idea that one day, someone would write a book about his experience.[88] In heaven, Job will discover that his story became a source of strength for many suffering believers. His trust in God during his time of trouble became a powerful apologetic. Job's story helped vindicate God's story.

Our stories can vindicate God's story too. When we're faced with suffering, *our trust in God* will speak volumes more than any oration or argument. Childlike faith is the best apologetic we can share.

More at the End

Scripture provides a detailed inventory of Job's family and property, both before and after the crisis.

Job 1 states that:

> "...his possessions were seven thousand sheep,
> three thousand camels,
> five hundred yoke of oxen,

---

[86] Job 2:9

[87] Job 13:15

[88] "An Introduction to the Book of Job," bible.org, n.d., https://bible.org/article/introduction-book-job

five hundred female donkeys
...And seven sons and three daughters were born to him"[89]

Let's compare these numbers to those of the final chapter of Job.

"Now the Lord blessed the latter days of Job more than his beginning;
for he had fourteen thousand sheep,
six thousand camels,
one thousand yoke of oxen,
one thousand female donkeys.
...and He also had seven sons and three daughters"[90]

By the end of the story, Job has twice as many sheep, camels, oxen, and donkeys as he did before. His riches are doubled, but he still has the same number of children he originally had.

Scholars have noted that the trajectory of the language seems to imply that, one day in heaven, Job will receive both sets of children. Job's ultimate restoration will be greater than his loss.

What Job lost will be returned to him in eternity.

In the grand finale, God *will* accomplish much more than merely a *recovery* from sin. Not only will heaven heal our hurts; it will exceed our wildest expectations.

Humanity will be brought into a closer and more favored relationship with God than if we had never sinned. Earth will become the capital of Heaven, and the Lord will reign with His people forever. Suffering and sorrow will end once and for all:

---

[89] Job 1:1-3
[90] Job 42:12-17

"Now I saw a new heaven and a new earth, for the first heaven and the first earth had passed away...Then I, John, saw the holy city, New Jerusalem, coming down out of heaven from God, prepared as a bride adorned for her husband. And I heard a loud voice from heaven saying, "Behold, the tabernacle of God is with men, and He will dwell with them, and they shall be His people. God Himself will be with them and be their God. And God will wipe away *every tear* from their eyes; there shall be no more death, nor sorrow, nor crying. There shall be no more pain, for the former things have passed away." (Revelation 21:1-4)

This is the ultimate solution God has promised. Does it answer all of our questions? *No.* But does it give us a good starting point? *Yes.*

In recapping, we can understand that the story of Job teaches several important lessons:
- A divine controversy is waging – a war between good and evil.
- Bad things happen to good people.
- Human answers are often insufficient for the problem of evil.
- God works to overcome evil with good.

Fellow believer, in times of darkness and weakness, Satan seeks to shake our hold upon God. But when you are in pain or experiencing great anxieties, put your life into the hands of Jesus and choose trust. He will not fail you. Abiding in God's love, you can stand every trial. Bring renewed faith in your experience. Faith will lighten every burden and will relieve every weariness. God will accomplish His purposes for you. He will not abandon you in your hour of need.

THINKING ABOUT THE PROBLEM OF EVIL:

- What does the word theodicy mean?

- What do most religions have in common?

- Why does love require freedom? Why is this so important to God?

- Are God and the devil equally powerful?

- What did God eventually bring out of Job's experience?

Chapter 7
Genocidal God or *Just* Judge?

In his book, *The God Delusion*, atheist Richard Dawkins wrote a vehement, unmitigated statement against the notion of a loving God. This statement has become a favorite amongst atheists:

> "The God of the Old Testament is arguably the most unpleasant character in all fiction: jealous and proud of it; a petty, unjust, unforgiving control-freak; a vindictive, bloodthirsty ethnic cleanser; a misogynistic, homophobic, racist, infanticidal, genocidal, filicidal, pestilential, megalomaniacal, sadomasochistic, capriciously malevolent bully."[91]

Dawkins' book sold millions of copies worldwide and is still considered a treasure by many atheists. While I don't agree with Dawkins' conclusions, the points he raised are important to address. His statement above criticizes the many documented wars and

---
[91] Richard Dawkins, The God Delusion (London Black Swan, 2016). Pg31

conquests that God commanded ancient Israel to engage in. Multiple times, God commanded the Israelites to wipe out their "enemies." The Biblical accounts of these events leave studious believers with many questions. Let's look at one such account:

> "Only in the cities of these peoples that the Lord your God is giving you as an inheritance, you shall not leave alive anything that breathes. But you shall utterly destroy them, the Hittite and the Amorite, the Canaanite and the Perizzite, the Hivite and the Jebusite, as the Lord your God has commanded you, so that they may not teach you to do according to all their detestable things which they have done for their gods, so that you would sin against the Lord your God." (Deut. 20:16-18)

Today, when we hear of civilians in war-torn countries being killed during drone attacks, or children being mowed down in gunfire; we are deeply disturbed – and rightly so. How then, can we understand God commanding Israel to do something that seems so similar? The idea that human beings – especially children – were killed during these divinely-ordained wars feels like a visceral gut punch.

What kind of God would command *that*?

I don't claim to fully understand this topic – a topic that should be approached with great humility and sensitivity. These events happened in the distant past. None of us were present to observe them. But I *do* think it's important to carefully think through these issues.

Not all careful thinkers have arrived at the same conclusions as Dawkins. While some of our questions won't be fully be answered until heaven, I believe God has revealed enough truth for us to continue trusting Him and His word in this life. With this in mind, let's examine the topic from some different angles. But first, a few more thoughts on Dawkins.

Atheists on Morality

As noted above, Richard Dawkins has sharply criticized God for being immoral, even claiming that belief in God is a "...bully."[92] But Dawkins has also claimed that objective morality doesn't even exist.

When author Larry Taunton asked Dawkins if his rejection of objective moral standards meant that Islamic terrorism might be justifiable, Dawkins replied, "What's to prevent us from saying Hitler wasn't right? I mean, that is a genuinely difficult question."[93]

Later on, Dawkins seemed to contradict himself, "Nobody wants to be caught agreeing with that monster [Hitler], even in a single particular."[94]

Reflecting on this contradiction, Mike Keas wrote, "On the one hand Dawkins (like all the rational and informed people I know) considers Hitler a moral monster. On the other hand, he proclaims that we can't rationally criticize Hitler's genocidal racism."[95]

Were Hitler's actions morally wrong or not? *Who gets to decide?*

Speaking of the ethics of eugenics, Dawkins tweeted, "Just as we breed cows to yield more milk, we could breed humans to run

---

[92] Dawkins p31

[93] Richard Weikart, The Death of Humanity: And the Case for Life (Washington, D.C.: Regnery Faith, 2016), 70.

[94] Mike Keas, "Richard Weikart on the Revealing Inconsistencies of Scientific Materialism," Evolution News, April 18, 2016, https://evolutionnews.org/2016/04/richard_weikart_2/

[95] Ibid.

faster or jump higher. But heaven forbid that we should do it."[96]

Heaven *forbid?*

Dawkins has argued that criminals are not responsible for their crimes, because they are like "defective machines," disadvantaged genetically, environmentally, etc. But, as professor Richard Weikart has pointed out, this notion of defectiveness "implies that somewhere there is a standard by which to measure human behavior, such as murder or rape. However, Dawkins's worldview does not have any moral resources to establish any standard he rightly recognizes that murder and rape are contrary to the way things should be. However, his commitment to materialism drives him to deny that there is any "way things should be."[97]

What we see here is an emerging bias against the Christian God. Sometimes Dawkins condemns God for His supposed immorality, but other times he seems to question whether morality even exists.

Well, which is it?

If no moral standards exist, it's invalid to claim anything is moral or immoral. Moral judgments require some kind of higher standard of right and wrong. If you believe theft is wrong merely because your society says it's wrong, you should remember that, in some societies, the act of stealing is seen as heroic. That's why we need something that transcends societal norms and individual feelings of right versus wrong. We need something objective. In the words of Frank Turek, "If there is no objective morality, then love is no better than murder."[98]

---

[96] Richard Dawkins, "Eugenics" Twitter, Feb 15, 2020.

[97] Ibid.

[98] Geisler, Norman L., and Frank Turek. 2004. I don't have enough faith to be an atheist. Wheaton, Ill: Crossway Books.

Where then can we *find* an objective moral standard?

If you reject theism, you are rejecting the basis for objective morality. When an atheist or agnostic condemns the notion of God as "unjust" and "vindictive," he or she is using a moral law to make such claims, but this moral law has to come from somewhere.

> "Where did Dawkins get the idea that cooperation, unselfishness, and generosity are *morally superior* to selfishness," Richard Weikart asks. "He admits that these moral precepts do not come from nature. Where then did he get these extra-natural (*dare I say, supernatural?*) moral standards that he encourages us to uphold and teach? They certainly did not arise from his own worldview."[99]

Next time you hear someone condemning God on the basis of His actions, ask this question: From where do you derive your universal basis of right and wrong? Where do you find the standard by which actions can be condemned or justified?

What about War?

Although Dawkins's claims are inconsistent, he's raised some important questions about the nature of God's character. Let's take some time to wrestle with this question of war.

The sixth commandment reads: *"thou shall not kill"* or *"you shall not murder."* The Hebrew word used here is ratsach, which literally means *"to dash into pieces, to murder, to be a (man) slayer."*

In our legal system, although taking life might be justified in some rare instances, murder can never be justified. Legally, the justification for taking life requires unique qualifications and circumstances. Murder, on the other hand, is the unjustified extermination of life based on unrighteous intentions. Jesus Himself

---

[99] Weikart, The Death of Humanity, 95.

compared murder with being *"angry without a cause,"* or angry without justification (Matthew 5:22).

Has God ever taken life? *Yes.*

Does God murder? *No.*

To do so, would make God a violator of His own law.

Military Lingo

A study of military literature from the ancient near east reveals something fascinating about the Old Testament accounts of war.

In Deuteronomy 7:2-5, Scripture indicates that God's people will *"utterly destroy"* the heathen nations, but then says *"you shall not intermarry among them."* This indicates that the biblical authors used a kind of rhetorical exaggeration (e.g., "all that breathes," "utterly destroy," etc.) familiar to other ancient Near East military accounts. This leaves open the possibility that these phrases may contain some degree of hyperbolic language, and thus, that non-combatants in these particular accounts may not have actually been killed.

In his book, *Is God a Moral Monster?*, evangelical author and theologian Paul Copan explains that *"Joshua used the rhetorical bravado language of his day, asserting that all the land was captured, all the kings defeated, and all the Canaanites destroyed."*[100] The point of his rhetoric was to assert God's total supremacy over the Canaanite idols. However, Joshua didn't believe that all the Canaanites had been destroyed (this is clear if you read the rest of the book of Joshua).

---

[100] Paul Copan, Is God a Moral Monster?: Making Sense of the Old Testament God (Grand Rapids, MI: Baker Books, 2011), 1–252.

"Just" War or "Just War"

Many philosophers have argued a *"just war"* ethic. When specific criteria for warfare is present, they claim, intervention might be justified. The question is: *what constitutes an appropriate use of force?*

History is replete with examples of what happens (or doesn't happen) when military intervention is (or isn't) utilized. Wars that some people have considered to be "just" (aka righteous or justifiable) have sometimes turned out to be anything but that. One example of this is the Rwandan genocide, when thousands of Tutsis were maliciously murdered by Hutu militia.

Convinced they were on the right side of history, the Hutu militia invaded villages, raped women, and killed anyone who identified as a Tutsi. Many Hutu civilians also joined in the bloodshed, arming themselves with machetes and clubs. The militia encouraged them to rape, maim, rob, and kill their Tutsi neighbors.[101] What they thought at the time was a *just war* ended up being *just a war* – a cruel and brutal conflict based on the desire to kill and conquer.

Did you know that the Bible actually articulates some important war time ethics? Moses, who had personally experienced the oppressive effects of Egypt's military system, instructed Israel that God wanted them to live by a more noble and righteous standard:

> "When you go near a city to fight against it, then proclaim an offer of peace to it. And it shall be that if they accept your offer of peace, and open to you, then all the people who are found in it shall be placed under tribute to you, and serve you..." (Deuteronomy 20:11-12)

---

[101] "Ignoring Genocide (HRW Report - Leave None to Tell the Story: Genocide in Rwanda, March 1999)," hrw.org, 2019, https://www.hrw.org/reports/1999/rwanda/Geno15-8-01.htm

> "When you go out to war against your enemies, and the Lord your God delivers them into your hand, and you take them captive, and you see among the captives a beautiful woman, and desire her and would take her for your wife...you may go in to her and be her husband, and she shall be your wife. And it shall be, if you have no delight in her, then you shall set her free, but you certainly shall not sell her for money; you shall not treat her brutally..." (Deuteronomy 21:10-14)

These wartime commands were designed to prevent Israel from turning into a brutal regime, wiping out anyone who stood in their way. An offer of peace was to be extended. Women were not to be enslaved or brutalized by the Israelite warriors. These ethics were very humane compared to the historically documented behavior[102] of other nations during this time period.

Cities or Military Outposts?

The assumptions we make about the hotspots of military conflicts in the Old Testament will influence the way we perceive those conflicts. If we imagine Jericho (Israel's first battle in Canaan) as a sprawling ancient city filled with schools, businesses, and homes, its destruction will seem unnecessarily brutal. But, as Joshua Ryan Butler explains in his book, *The Skeletons in God's Closet*, this perception isn't accurate:

> "The cities Israel takes out are military *strongholds*, not civilian population centers...So when Israel 'utterly destroys' a city like Jericho or Ai, we should picture a military fort being taken over – not a civilian massacre. God is pulling down the Great Wall of China, not demolishing Beijing. Israel is taking out the Pentagon, not New York City."[103]

---

[102] Berry, George R. "The Ethical Teaching of the Old Testament." The Biblical World 21, no. 2 (1903): 108-14. Accessed April 29, 2021.

[103] Joshua Ryan Butler, The Skeletons in God's Closet: The Mercy of Hell, the Surprise of Judgment, the Hope of Holy War (Nashville, TN: Thomas Nelson, 2014).

This information doesn't remove all the difficult questions, but it does begin to clarify the context. God gave strategic commands to Israel to destroy specific cities that the Canaanites used as defensive military outposts.

Notice the language in Joshua's description of Jericho, "Now Jericho was securely shut up because of the children of Israel; none went out, and none came in. And the Lord said to Joshua, "See! I have given Jericho into your hand, *its king, and the mighty men of valor*." (Joshua 6:1, emphasis my own)

Geographical vs. Racial Motivation

Shortly before Israel entered the holy land, Moses gave them guidelines for warfare. This instruction was highly significant since they were about to enter into conflict:

> "...The Lord your God brings you into the land which you go to possess, and has cast out many nations before you, the Hittites and the Girgashites and the Amorites and the Canaanites and the Perizzites and the Hivites and the Jebusites, seven nations greater and mightier than you." (Deuteronomy 7:1-2)

This passage is crucial to understand. Moses pointed out several pagan nations that had inhabited the land of Canaan. Why did they need to be displaced? Not because of their race, but because of geography.

God had chosen Canaan for His people because it was located in the proverbial *"heart"* of the populated world:

> "Canaan was at the crossroads of the world, forming a bridge between three continents: Asia to the east, Africa to the south, and Europe to the north. It was a meeting place for the highly

developed civilizations from Egypt and Babylon...Across the sea, Canaan was a trade center for towns all around the Mediterranean as well as being the connection via the Red Sea between the Mediterranean and the Indian Ocean."[104]

This special landmass was the crossroads of the then-known world. Everyone knew someone from Canaan or someone connected to Canaan. The divine plan was to bring Israel into this area, establishing a place of worship and influence. Why? So the surrounding nations would see the goodness of God's principles and come to trust in the Messiah who would eventually come through Abraham's lineage.

This helps us better understand God's motivation in conquest. The wars of the Old Testament were geographically, not racially, motivated. God knew that constant pagan influences and interruptions in the Promised Land would hinder His plan to bless the entire world. But He didn't command His people to attack people of these particular nations throughout the world. He never intended to completely destroy other ethnicities. On the contrary, the reason why God brought Israel into Canaan was so they could be "a light to the Gentiles," revealing God's salvation "to the ends of the earth" (Isaiah 49:6). God's ultimate goal was to save rather than destroy.

The Real Enemy

Several years ago, I had the privilege of walking through the rubble of ancient Jericho on an archeological tour. Jericho was an imposing fortress to anyone who dared to cross into the land.

---

[104] Ben Hobrink, Modern Science in the Bible: Amazing Scientific Truths Found in Ancient Texts (New York: Howard Books, 2011).

The book of Joshua tells the story of the Israelites awaiting their marching orders against Jericho with bated breath. Joshua, God's chosen commander of the people, walked off by himself to contemplate this decisive battle. Soon, a powerful, armor-clad Warrior stood before him in dazzling brightness:

> "...And Joshua went to Him and said to Him, *'Are you for us or for our adversaries?'*
>
> So He said, *'No, but as Commander of the army of the Lord, I have now come.'*
>
> And Joshua fell on his face to the earth and worshiped..." (Joshua 5:13-15)

God showed up to give Joshua tactical instructions. But He said something surprising. Joshua had asked a straightforward question:

> *Are you for us or these pagans? ...Which team? Which nation? Which religion?*

God's response in Joshua 1:14 was...*No*

...*No?*

Joshua was expecting a simple affirmation that God was on his side. But God gave a profound answer to this simple question: *"Joshua, this battle isn't about your nation versus theirs or your team versus theirs. Something else is going on here."* Joshua's understanding was limited, but there was another agenda at work – a *divine agenda*. God wanted the destruction of Canaanite wickedness more than the destruction of the Canaanites themselves.

Love Warns

God deals fairly with individuals, groups, societies, and nations. Scripture contains many examples of God giving mercy and opportunity for repentance.

During Abraham's time, God chose not to remove the Amorites (another pagan people). He said *"the sins of the Amorites do not yet warrant their destruction"* (Genesis 15:16). Instead, they were given more time to change their selfish ways. Heaven alone will reveal God's many attempts to redeem the Amorites during that time. But they were insistent in their ways, refusing to change.

Centuries later, when Moses and the Israelites traveled close to the Holy Land, the Amorites attacked God's nomadic people without provocation (Numbers 21:21-35). Their violent, aggressive acts revealed that intervention was necessary. The Amorites were eventually destroyed in the conquest of Canaan. Once God saw that they were incorrigible and would harm His people, their time of probation ended.

> ***God constantly warned people in order to protect them from the damaging results of their own selfish decisions.***

Notice the sequence:

- Abraham was told of the Amorites (Genesis 15:16).
- The Amorites were given a probation period of several hundred years.
- The Amorites didn't reform, but became aggressive towards peaceful groups (Numbers 21:21).
- Intervention took place (Numbers 21:35).

The story of Sodom and Gomorrah also reveals God's compassion for anyone willing to repent. When the Lord and His angels investigated the city of Sodom, Abraham was allowed to plead for the nation. If only five righteous people were in the city, God promised not to destroy it (Genesis 18).

But five righteous people couldn't be found. The citizens of Sodom and Gomorrah were bent on evil. They even attempted to rape their angelic guests (Genesis 19). This act was symptomatic of the widespread violence, greed, and corruption that had overtaken the city.

When the rights of the innocent and vulnerable are abused and trampled upon, the Lord of Heaven ultimately deals justly with those who are guilty and beyond reformation. This is why Abraham says, "*shall not the Judge of the earth do right...*" (Genesis 18:25).

In His mercy, God allowed the only three people in the city who still showed integrity to escape the destruction.

Back to Jericho

What was happening in Jericho before its destruction? Was it as wicked as Sodom and Gomorrah? A well-known Old Testament commentary points out that "Jericho was one of the *principal seats* of idol worship, being especially devoted to Ashtoreth, the moon's goddess. Here centered all that was vilest and most degrading in the religion of the Canaanites."[105]

What was so vile and degrading? In short, it was widespread prostitution and child sacrifice. According to one account,

---

[105] Ibid.

"Sacred or cultic prostitution was practiced in order to ensure the fertility of the land. Fertility of the field, flock, and family was thought to depend upon the sexual relations between Baal and Anath (or Asherah)... Thus male and female worshipers engaged in sacred sexual acts in the temple in order to assure for themselves the blessings of nature. Another practice associated with Canaanite holy places was child sacrifice. Children were offered to the Canaanite gods as the supreme sacrifice and as a demonstration of faith by the worshiper."[106]

The scene in Jericho was grotesque, but it seems that God was much more angry with the corrupt system that perpetuated prostitution than with the vulnerable people who were exploited by it. We see this in the story of Rahab, who had been a harlot in Jericho.

Rahab was the lone survivor of the Jericho war (Joshua 2-6) and an eventual convert to Israel's religion. Rahab married a Jew and gave birth to a bouncing baby boy named Boaz. This boy grew up and fell in love with Ruth, a convert from a pagan land (just like Boaz's mother). Perhaps there's truth to the old proverb, *"Men marry women like their mothers."*

Why am I telling this story? Because Ruth and Boaz were the great-grandparents of King David, which means that Christ also came from their lineage. God placed a former prostitute in His own family tree. Today, He still abhors sex trafficking and abuse of every kind.

Child Sacrifice

The Bible tells us that Joshua conquered a variety of cities in Canaan. In Joshua 10:33, we read one of these accounts:

---

[106] Claude Mariottini, "Canaan in Patriarchal Times – Part 1," Dr. Claude Mariottini, November 9, 2006, https://claudemariottini.com/2006/11/09/canaan-in-patriarchal-times-part-1/

"Then Horam king of Gezer came up to help Lachish; and Joshua struck him and his people, until he left him none remaining."

Why was this particular group targeted? Archaeologists have discovered that something very disturbing was happening in Gezer:

"Under the sanctuary in the ancient city of Gezer, urns containing the *burnt* bones of children have been found that are dated to somewhere between 2000 and 1500 BC, between the time of Abraham and the Exodus."[107]

Child sacrifice was not an isolated practice. In 1921, the largest cemetery of sacrificed infants in the ancient Near East was discovered in Carthage, a former outpost of worship to the Canaanite god Moloch.

It is well established that the rite of child sacrifice originated in Phoenicia, ancient Israel's northern neighbor. This despicable practice was brought to Carthage by Phoenician colonizers. In the ruins of Carthage, archaeologists have uncovered hundreds of burial urns filled with cremated bones, mostly of infants, but also of children up to six years old.

What motivated this cruelty? "Therefore, the Carthaginians, believing that the misfortune had come to them from the gods, betook themselves to every manner of supplication of the divine power," one ancient historian wrote. "In their zeal to make amends for their omission, they selected two hundred of the noblest children and *sacrificed* them publicly." [108]

---

[107] James Orr, 550.

[108] Siculus Diodorus and Francis R. Walton, Diodorus of Sicily: Fragments of Books XXI - XXXII (Cambridge, MA: Harvard Univ. Press, 1980).

Plutarch, the ancient Greek philosopher and historian, also reflected on this devious worship:

> "There was in their city a bronze image of Cronus extending its hands, palms up and sloping toward the ground so that each of the children when placed thereon rolled down and fell into a sort of gaping pit filled with fire...The whole area before the statue was filled with a loud noise of flutes and drums so that the *cries of wailing* [of the children being sacrificed] should not reach the ears of the people."[109]

Child sacrifice was such a recurrent problem that, in the book of Jeremiah, written approximately centuries after the Israelites entered Canaan, God was still speaking against it: "And they have built the high places of Tophet,... to burn their sons and their daughters in the fire, which I did not command, nor did it come into My heart" (Jeremiah 7:31).

Lawrence E. Stager, archaeology professor and director of the Semitic Museum at Harvard University, points out that the child cemetery in Carthage (called the *Tophet*) holds an estimated 20,000 urns.[110]

When I toured areas of ancient Israel, my archaeology professor pointed out the remains of altars used to sacrifice children. The other students and I paused in horror – there was nothing to say. In the heart of the land of God's own people, this vile practice gained a foothold multiple times.

---

[109] Plutarch, De Superstitione (Milano: Cisalpino-Goliardica, 1980).

[110] Lawrence Stager, "Child Sacrifice in Carthage: Religious Rite or Population Control?," Journal of Biblical Archeological Review 10, no. 1 (January 1984): 31–46.

Unfortunately, child sacrifice has historical roots all over the world. According to anthropologist Laila Williamson, "Infanticide has been practiced on every continent and by people on every level of cultural complexity, from hunter-gatherers to high civilizations, including our own ancestors. Rather than being an exception, then, it has been the rule." [111]

This horrendous rite was supposed to be abolished in Canaan through the destruction of its proponents, but its ugly head repeatedly reemerged. It seems that the devilish agenda behind child sacrifice was to attack the truth of the gospel (in addition to murdering the children).

If the devil could lead people to believe that their children's blood would appease the gods, they would view the true God as harsh and vindictive — requiring a human sacrifice rather than providing a Sacrifice.

This potent deception permeated many ancient cultures and religions.

Abraham and Isaac

God wanted to disabuse His people of the notion of child sacrifice. Surrounded by nations that were trying to appease the gods, they were at risk of misunderstanding God's character. With this in mind, God chose a creative and counterintuitive way to teach His people what He was *really* like.

Genesis 22 tells us that God commanded Abraham to *sacrifice* his only son Isaac. You can imagine how shocked Abraham must have been

---

[111] Marvin Kohl, Infanticide and the Value of Life (Buffalo, NY: Prometheus Books, 1978), 61–75.

to hear God demand the same thing the pagan gods supposedly demanded. How could God want the blood of his dear son, Isaac?

In reality, God never wanted Isaac's blood. After Abraham climbed a mountain, placed Isaac on the altar, and raised His knife to sacrifice his only son, God dramatically prevented him from carrying out the deed:

> "But the Angel of the Lord called to him from heaven and said, 'Abraham, Abraham!' So he said, 'Here I am.' And He said, 'Do not lay your hand on the lad, or do anything to him…' Then Abraham lifted his eyes and looked, and there behind him was a ram *caught in a thicket* by its horns. So Abraham went and took the ram, and offered it up for a burnt offering instead of his son" (Genesis 22:11-13).

God provided a ram that day for Abraham. The ram took the place of Isaac, revealing a powerful lesson about redemption. It represented Jesus, who would one day offer himself as a Substitute for mankind. This story, which took place in the land of Canaan, was to be an influential reminder that God never required human sacrifice. The Israelites were to share this lesson with the world. If they had been faithful to their mission, they might have helped prevent child sacrifice in many places.

Before Abraham and his son had climbed the mountain, Isaac noticed that the usual sacrificial lamb was missing: "Look, the fire and the wood, but where is the lamb for a burnt offering?" he asked (Genesis 22:7). Abraham had not yet told Isaac about God's heartbreaking request. With a heavy heart, Abraham simply said to his son, *"God will provide."*[112]

---

[112] Gen. 22:8

God has provided His only Son for humanity. That's the message of the gospel and the message of God's Old Testament sanctuary/sacrificial system. Satan tried to destroy this message by clouding people's minds with the pagan practice of child sacrifice.

Would Satan use such atrocious means to make God appear cruel? Would he attempt to distort the Plan of Redemption symbols?

You can bet your money on it.

Public Health Threats

As someone fascinated by public health, I've studied various models of how to contain disease in case of an outbreak. The COVID-19 pandemic gave our world a crash course in the successes and failures of various disease containment protocols.

We've already discussed some of the dangers of Canaanite culture, but there's more to the story. The lifestyle habits of some of the Canaanites represented a severe public health threat to the Israelites. While additional research is needed on this topic, I believe it's an important point to consider.

Some of the more dangerous health issues were various diseases (such as parasitic), which ravaged many of Canaan's inhabitants, especially sexually transmitted diseases and numerous plagues. Diseases of this type spread most easily in countries where people have low social status and poor hygiene. These were precisely the conditions of Canaan. The low life expectancy of around thirty years at the time demonstrated the devastating effects of these diseases.

God gave the children of Israel many public health instructions that were far ahead of the time. This included guidelines for proper nutrition (Leviticus 11), waste management (Deuteronomy

23:12-13), hygiene, quarantine, burial, etc. God's health principles were so effective that nearly two thousand years later, conscientious Jews had much lower rates of infection during the Black Plague than did the general population.[113] Of course, that didn't mean they were entirely without risk. The same was true in the days of Moses. Regardless of how carefully the children of Israel followed God's health instructions, close association with infected people was dangerous, especially since the Israelites lived in such a close-knit community. [114]

The radical measures God took to protect the people of Israel may seem overly stringent. But if God hadn't commanded this, countless Israelites would have died in appalling conditions due to sexually transmitted diseases and deadly epidemics. Ultimately, with the strict rules, it's likely that many more lives were spared than were lost in the death of the Canaanites

Leviticus 15 offers multiple guidelines to prevent the spread of what appears to be some type of transmissible disease(s). Since no documented diagnostic methods were reported, and no known cure for venereal disease was available, these written preventive measures were designed to avert an epidemic. This topic would only have been necessary for Moses to write about if the danger was actually present. Does this justify certain measures against the Canaanites?

No.

Does it add more details to the context? Yes.

---

[113] Pasachoff, Naomi E.; Littman, Robert J. (2005). A Concise History of the Jewish People. Lanham: Rowman & Littlefield. p. 154

[114] Ibid.

What Were God's Options?

It's easy to claim that God shouldn't have directed military conquests in the Old Testament. But perhaps we should stop to consider what would have happened if He had done nothing.

There are several examples in the book of Joshua of times when the Israelites failed to carry out God's instructions to destroy certain nations, sometimes even succumbing to their evil influences. This decision always came back to haunt them.

After King Saul failed to conquer the Amalekites, their descendants eventually threatened to exterminate God's people. This story is recorded in the book of Esther: "Haman, the son of Hammedatha the Agagite[115], the enemy of all the Jews, had plotted against the Jews to destroy them..." (Esther 9:24) Haman was a descendent of the Amalekites.

It seems that if God had taken a more passive approach to the Canaanites, he would have risked the safety, health, spirituality, and very existence of Israel – the people through whom the Savior would come.

God's Covenantal Plan

God had promised to bring the Messiah through the lineage of Abraham. This covenant was of utmost importance. Without its fulfillment, humanity could not be saved. To protect the lineage of the Messiah, God sometimes had to place pagan nations and tribes in check.

But God also *used* pagan nations to discipline Israel.

---

[115] from Agag who was king of the Amalekites

When the children of Israel failed to honor God's covenant agreement, they were not immune to His judgments. Examples of this include the Babylonian and Assyrian captivities. In Deuteronomy 28, God warned Israel, "*The LORD will bring a nation against you from afar, from the end of the earth, as swift as the eagle flies, a nation whose language you will not understand.*" In other places, He called Assyria "His rod" to correct.[116]

Although God had a special plan for Israel, He did not intend on spoiling or enabling them at the expense of the genuine welfare of others.

Were the Other Nations Eternally Lost?

Some people assume that every person who met God's judgments in the Old Testament will be eternally lost. But at times, Scripture seems to differentiate between certain people *dying* in judgment versus being *lost* in the judgment.

For example, many Israelites perished in the wilderness because of their unbelief and sins. This included Miriam (Numbers 20:1), Aaron the high priest (Numbers 33:39), and even Moses (Deuteronomy 34). Because of divine judgment, none of them made it into the Holy Land. But we know Moses was resurrected (Jude 9), and the others will be redeemed as well. It's not always precisely clear to us who will be lost or saved after earthly judgment events.

Describing the future glory of heaven, one of the psalmists wrote something fascinating:

> "Glorious things are spoken of you, O city of God! 'I will make mention of Rahab and Babylon to those who know Me; Behold, O Philistia and Tyre, with Ethiopia: This one was born there.'

---

[116] Isa. 10:5

And of Zion, it will be said, 'This one and that one were born in her, And the Most High Himself shall establish her.' The Lord will record, When He registers the peoples: 'This one was born there.'" (Psalm 87:3-6)

In this prophetic glimpse into eternity, the psalmist apparently hears the roll call of Zion (the city of God) and learns about the birthplaces of its citizens. *Philistia? Tyre? Babylon?* These groups were considered to be the mortal enemies of ancient Israel. But some people from these groups will be citizens of God's kingdom!

Despite the wickedness existing in these nations, there was a few who were still open to God's Spirit and willing to heed the convictions of their consciences (Romans 2:14-15).

In Conclusion

Although many questions remain, I hope this chapter has provided food for thought on a very difficult topic. I believe God blesses our efforts to seek truth and to understand the context of His Word.

There are some things we will never completely understand on this side of eternity. What we can't comprehend, we can leave with God, awaiting more clarification in a future conversation. In the meantime, we can be open to the possibility of God's mercy and goodness even in the darkest of stories.

One day, God's wisdom, His justice, and His goodness will stand fully vindicated. The entire universe will admit that all of God's dealings with this world were conducted for the *eternal good* of His people and of all His creation.

"All Thy works shall praise Thee, O Lord; and Thy saints shall bless Thee" (Psalm 145:10).

THINKING ABOUT ANCIENT CONQUESTS:

- What must exist in order for us to call something evil or good?

- What was one of the rules of war Moses gave to the Israelites?

- What evil practices were happening in the land of Canaan?

- Why is the story of Abraham and Isaac so important?

- What kind of people will be in heaven?

Chapter 8
Abraham's *Other* Children:
How God Works With Other Nations

As the old man looked up at the stars glimmering in the night sky, God spoke to him:

> "...I will multiply your descendants as the stars of the heaven and as the sand which is on the seashore; and your descendants shall possess the gate of their enemies. In your seed, all the nations of the earth shall be blessed, because you have obeyed My voice" (Genesis 22:17-18).

Abraham was told the nations of the world would be blessed through his lineage. What a marvelous promise! The name of Abraham, which means "father of many," is revered in many lands and by many faiths, including Judaism, Christianity, and Islam. The life of this old patriarch stands as a record of faithfulness, obedience, and trust in God.

Our planet is currently home to roughly 7.8 billion people who come from multiple faith backgrounds, including:

Christianity	2.4 billion[117]
Islam	1.9 billion
Hinduism	1.15 billion
Buddhism	521 million
Sikhism	30 million
Judaism	14.5 million
Baha'i'	7.0 million
Jainism	4.2 million
Universalism	0.8 million

Although roughly a third of the world's population identifies as Christian, the majority of Christians subscribe to certain beliefs that significantly vary from those found in Scripture. In addition, only a small minority of Christians in our world are actively engaged in sharing the gospel.

This context raises some very important questions:

How does God work to save the nations when there are so few missionaries and so much confusion in religion? How does He judge those who lived in a place or time in which the news of the gospel never reached them? What about the nations not mentioned in the Bible? Did God work to help them too?

---

[117] Michael Lipka, "7 Key Changes in the Global Religious Landscape," Pew Research Center (, April 2, 2015), https://www.pewresearch.org/fact-tank/2015/04/02/7-key-changes-in-the-global-religious-landscape/

I wrestled hard with these questions before becoming a Christian. I come from a land whose major religion is Hinduism – not Christianity. India is also the birthplace of Buddhism, and has been influenced by Islam. Had it not split into modern-day India and Pakistan, it might currently be the country with the most Muslims. India is a land of deep cultural and religious roots, which go back thousands of years.

I believe in Bible truth. I believe Jesus is the way to the Father and our only perfect Sacrifice. I see many compelling reasons to accept the claims of the Bible. But I have relatives who have never had Biblical truths clearly explained to them. My family history goes back hundreds of years without a single documented conversion to Christianity. This explains why one of the most significant barriers to my faith was the question of why the God of the Bible was so exclusive.

If God loves every human being, but salvation comes through faith in Christ, how are we to understand God's care for unreached people groups?

Does God work with these people? Does He answer the prayers of sincere, god-fearing Hindus, Buddhists, and Muslims? Does He work in their lives as much as He has in mine?

My Uncle

As I drove home from a church event one Saturday afternoon, my family called to tell me my uncle had passed away. Our families were very close as I grew up. I have many fond memories of my uncle, who often had kind words for me. He was a spiritual man, involved with the Radha Swami Beas fellowship. A gentle-hearted man, he spent hours in meditation.

After I became a Christian, my uncle was curious about my new faith. He occasionally asked questions and nodded in agreement as I shared what I knew. I had hoped that one day he would come to know the Lord as I have. When I heard the tragic news, I had to pull my car over to gather my thoughts. *How could this be? I wondered, Is there no Savior for these people? Do they not have any hope?*

The next day, I providentially came across a devotional writing that explained how God works with other people groups. It was written by Ellen White, a former abolitionist, social activist, health reformer, theological thinker, and author – one of the most broadly translated female authors (of non-fiction) in the history of literature. White was recognized by The Smithsonian as one of the most significant Americans of all time.[118] I've been blessed by her writings, and this instance was no exception. She beautifully described God's heart for all people groups:

> "Heaven's plan of salvation is broad enough to embrace the whole world And God *will not* permit any soul to be disappointed who is sincere in his longing for something higher and nobler than anything the world can offer. Constantly He is sending His angels to those who, while surrounded by circumstances the most discouraging, pray in faith for some power higher than themselves to take possession of them and bring deliverance and peace. In various ways, *God will reveal Himself* to them and will place them in touch with providences that will establish their confidence in the One who has given Himself a ransom for all."[119]

---

[118] Michael Lipka, "7 Key Changes in the Global Religious Landscape," Pew Research Center (, April 2, 2015), https://www.pewresearch.org/fact-tank/2015/04/02/7-key-changes-in-the-global-religious-landscape/

[119] Ellen G. White, The Story of Prophets and Kings as Illustrated in the Captivity and Restoration of Israel (Mountain View, CA: Pacific Press Publishing, 1917).

Notice those key phrases:

- "Heaven's plan of salvation is *broad enough* to embrace the whole world."

- "God will not permit any soul to be disappointed who is sincere in his longing for something higher."

- "He is sending His angels to those who...pray in faith for *some power* higher than themselves."

- "In various ways, God will *reveal* Himself to them."

This understanding of God is much broader and more loving in its scope than many people realize. God works with every human being in various ways and through multiple means. He ministers to them in the way they understand best. Scripture gives us the clearest and most accurate revelation of God, but God also knows how to communicate with those who don't have access to it. Let's examine this further.

Jesus is called the true light. John, whose gospel was written for the Gentiles, wrote:

"That was the true Light which gives light to every man coming into the world" (John 1:9).

These words indicate that knowledge about God is given to all human beings in some way. John doesn't state here *how much* knowledge is given, or *how* it is given, but the apostle Paul provides further insight:

"For since the creation of the world God's invisible qualities – his eternal power and divine nature – have been clearly seen, being understood from what has been made, so that men are without excuse" (Romans 1:20).

Paul says that Gentiles (non-Jews) are not left without a witness of God, because they are given His created works to help them recognize His goodness. Paul argues that all humans are accountable for the light God has revealed to them:

"For as many as have sinned without law will also perish without law, and as many as have sinned in the law will be judged by the law (for not the hearers of the law are just in the sight of God, but the doers of the law will be justified; for when Gentiles, who do not have the law, by nature do the things in the law, these, although not having the law, are a law to themselves, who show the work of the law written in their hearts, their conscience also bearing witness, and between themselves their thoughts accusing or else excusing them)" (Romans 2:12-15).

Each of us will be judged by whether we lived up to the light we received — whether it was a little light or great light. Individuals and cultural groups who never had a single Bible or missionary reach them will be judged according to their response to however much light was given to them. They will be judged by whether they tried to lived up to what they knew of the loving character of God. Every human being is tested according to the specific light they receive.

- No one will be lost simply because of ignorance.
- No one will be lost simply because of where they were born.
- No one will be lost simply because of what truth they could or could not access.
- No one will be lost simply because they were born in the wrong time period.

Many scholars believe that Scripture predicts a beautiful scene in the future when some of these honest "outsiders" get to heaven and encounter Christ:

> "And one shall say unto him, What are these wounds in thine hands?" (Zechariah 13:6)

Apparently, some people will arrive in heaven to discover a Messiah with wounds in His hands. Their question to Him indicates that they don't know the salvation story. How will Christ respond?

> "Then he shall answer, Those with which I was wounded in the house of My friends" (Zechariah 13:6).

It seems that many people will hear the gospel story for the first time in heaven. These people will discover their Savior *after* being saved. Like all the redeemed, they will only be saved by God's grace, but the choices they made in their lives revealed that their hearts were open to His influence of love.

What About Missionaries (or lack thereof)?

The human missionary is God's *modus operandi*, His preferred method, for spreading the gospel to the world. In Christ's parting words to the disciples, He said: "Go therefore and make disciples of all the nations, baptizing them in the name of the Father and of the Son and of the Holy Spirit, teaching them to observe all things that I have commanded you..." (Matthew 28:18-20).

God's ideal is that human beings will share the gospel with the world. But He isn't *limited* by human beings. If, through neglect or extenuating circumstances, no missionary reaches the poor souls or groups struggling for light in deprived areas of the world, our merciful God has a *modus vivendi* (a feasible arrangement), a plan B to bypass what would otherwise be a fatal hindrance to salvation.

God loves to use human beings as His witnesses, in part because He knows their faith will grow as they share it. But He is not limited by them. God has infinite means at His disposal to communicate His grace and truth.

Throughout history, God has used everything from dreams, the weather, fish, plants, stars, and even donkeys to communicate His lessons. Jesus said that if human beings were silent, "the very stones would cry out" (Luke 19:39-40). Aside from miraculous methods, He also speaks through the still small voices of our consciences. God gives light to every human being. It's up to them whether or not they will accept or reject the grace He offers.

White described this point in more detail:

> "Among the heathen are those who worship God ignorantly, those to whom the light is never brought by human instrumentality, yet they will not perish. Though ignorant of the written law of God, *they have heard* His voice speaking to them in nature and have done the things that the law required. Their works are evidence that the Holy Spirit has touched their hearts, and they are recognized as the children of God."[120]

What a relief to know that our loving God works to save everyone He possibly can.

Abraham's Other Son

Our world is home to approximately two billion Muslims. Many live in countries where proselytizing is illegal, often even punishable by death. Although Muslims revere the memory of Abraham, their theology contains a significant twist in his story.

Scripture clearly states that Isaac was Abraham's promised son—the one through whom the Messiah would come and all nations

---

[120] Ellen G. White, The Desire of Ages: The Conflict of the Ages Illustrated in the Life of Christ, (Mountain View, CA, Portland, OR: Pacific Press Pub. Association, 1947), 238.

would be blessed. Abraham and Sarah doubted God's promise of a son because they were so old. For this reason, Abraham slept with Sarah's servant Hagar in order to produce an heir. Hagar gave birth to a son named Ishmael, assuming he was the promised son (Genesis 16).

But God had a greater purpose in mind. He wanted to show Abraham and Sarah that He could keep His promises despite human limitations. Sarah eventually became pregnant and gave birth to Isaac – the heir God had promised (Genesis 21).

Although Scripture is clear on the subject, Muslim theology teaches that Ishmael – not Isaac – was the promised son. Muslim's trace their connection to Abraham through Ishmael. They believe Muhammad was a descendant of Ishmael, set apart by God to establish a great nation. Although this belief contradicts the Bible and denies the divinity of Christ, it's true that God cared about Abraham's "other" son. God even instructed Hagar to name the boy Ishmael, which means "God hears" (Genesis 16). Ishmael, a man considered to be a spiritual father to Muslims everywhere, was specifically named by God.

God hears? *Yes.*

Embedded in that name was a symbol of hope for a future people who would multiply exceedingly.

Somewhere, even now, an honest-hearted Muslim is praying for help from a merciful God. Ishmael's story shows us that the Lord will not abandon any of His children who sincerely plead for help.

Yes, God hears

The God of the Bible reaches out in unique ways to every mind and heart. Only in light of eternity will we understand the providences of God and recognize how interested He was in our salvation.

How marvelous it will be to arrive in heaven and see the people of Nineveh, the wise men from the East, Naaman the Syrian, Cornelius the centurion, the Queen of Sheba, the Syrophoenician woman who prayed to God, and many others who followed the divine light. We likely also will encounter some individuals throughout history who rejected Christianity due to poor theology or spiritual abuse, but never rejected the truth that God revealed to them.

When God pointed Abraham to the glorious starry sky as symbolic of his numerous descendants, He had salvation in mind for all kinds of people.

What About Universalism?

The facts above lead to an undeniable conclusion. *God is inclusive.* But does this mean *everyone* will be in heaven? Some believe so. Universalism is the philosophical belief that all people will ultimately be saved regardless of their beliefs, thoughts, choices, and actions.

At first glance, this perspective sounds loving. The idea that some people will be lost strikes universalists as exclusive and judgmental. But a closer look reveals that something is seriously wrong with this perspective.

- Universalism removes freedom of choice.
- Universalism diminishes the justice of God.
- Universalism minimizes the importance of faith and spirituality.
- Universalism renders the gospel unnecessary.
- Universalism ignores many passages in Scripture.

Although this belief has infiltrated some Christian circles, it's ultimately founded on erroneous presuppositions. The plan of redemption started because of a rebellion in heaven. If people who repeatedly choose evil in this life are allowed in heaven, what would prevent another rebellion from occurring?

Part of the ultimate salvation of the universe is God's eradication of sin once and for all. This message is particularly comforting to victims of abuse and mistreatment. God promises to execute judgment and protect His people from danger.

If God could save everyone regardless of whether they accepted His sacrifice (to the extent that they knew how), why would Christ's death have been necessary?

Scripture teaches that in the end, evil people find God's presence to be torturous, crying out for the rocks and mountains to fall on them (Revelation 6:16). How could these same people enjoy an eternity in God's presence, living in an environment ruled by unselfish love? Believers would have to ignore many passages in Scripture (and misinterpret others) in order to embrace universalism.

Does God want everyone to be saved? Yes. John 3:16 answers that question. Will He violate people's free will to save them? *No.*

People have to decide what to do with the grace offered to them. They can reject it and be lost forever or believe and let God transform their hearts.

Here are some key thoughts to recap this chapter:

- God loves everyone and wants as many as possible to be saved (2 Peter 3:9).

- God works with every human being in a wide variety of ways. He is not dependent on human instrumentalities (1 King 19:11-13).

- No one is saved apart from the gospel. Its virtue is applied to all who desire redemption and deliverance from sin, even if they don't fully understand the gospel story (Romans 5:19).

- Divine light is given to all. What people decide to do with that light will be the criterion of judgment (John 3:19). God will honor the choices of those who accept His grace, as well as those who reject it.

Christmas Light

I love the Christmas season (even if you don't).

Here's why.

I did not grow up in a Christian household, but around December my father would place tiny statues of the nativity scene right by the Christmas tree. Sometimes, he would have us watch movies about Jesus playing on television during that time. I can recognize looking back, the Spirit was revealing Christ to my family.

Take a look at what the angel said to the shocked shepherds on the day Christ was born:

> *But the angel reassured them. "Don't be afraid!" he said. "I bring you good news that will bring great joy to all people (Luke 2:10)*

Look at the components of that message:

Good news. Great joy. *All people.*

Let me *repeat* that.

Good news. Great joy. *All people.*

Be careful of a religion that proposes a gospel that isn't those three things.

The blood of Jesus is available to anyone and everyone. Jesus died for the *whole world* because He believed every single person (Christian, Jew, Hindu, Sikh, Muslim, Buddhist, etc.) was worth dying for and capable of receiving His grace.

For God so loved the world ... (John 3:16)

That's good news.

I'm here because of that. So are you.

THINKING ABOUT GOD'S INCLUSIVITY:

- How does God work with people who haven't heard or understood the gospel?

- What is universalism and why is it problematic?

- On what basis are people judged?

- What will surprise many of the redeemed when they get to heaven?

- What does the name Ishmael mean? Why is this significant?

Chapter 9
So, You Want to be an Apologist?

Regardless of your faith background, I hope you've enjoyed the book so far.

I love sharing apologetics. I can't help myself. What about you? Is your faith worth explaining and defending?

The next few chapters are written for readers who want to share their faith more effectively. You don't have to be a theologian or pastor in order to make a difference. Some of the best apologists are ordinary people.

Apologists are *paradigm shifters* who work to help their friends, family members, classmates, coworkers, and even strangers. They seek to remove intellectual and emotional barriers to faith so people can see the beauty of God and His truth.

You can be an apologist! Whether in the classroom, your church, your workplace, or a neighborhood coffee shop, you can reach others with the good news of Jesus Christ.

> *The goal is to know what you believe,*
> *why you believe it, and*
> *how to communicate those beliefs with others.*

Sharing your faith will likely help you just as much as anyone else. The best way to learn something is to teach it. Apologetics will help you become more confident in what you believe and why. It will remind you of God's goodness and enhance your sense of purpose. Personally, I've found there's no greater joy than sharing God's love with others.

Clearing Up the Confusion

Believers have something infinitely valuable to offer the world. But God has been seriously misrepresented. Many false teachings have crept into the culture and the church. Because of the darkness and confusion, many people don't want to have anything to do with the God of the Bible.

Scripture actually predicted this would happen. The book of Revelation calls this confused state of Christianity "Babylon," and begs God's people to "come out" of it.[121] Apologists have a special role to play in the final events of earth's history. We are called to speak clarity into the confusion. In order to do this effectively, we need to understand the beliefs and objections of those we are working with.

---

[121] Rev. 18:4

Let's take a look at some of the beliefs of young people today. Of course, people of all ages need apologetics, but I'd like to spend a little time focusing on the younger generation.

The Justice Generation

According to Pew Research Center, each generation is less interested in religion than the generation before it. Generation Z is the least-religious generation.[122] Many consider themselves to be "spiritual," but not religious.

Millennials and GenZs feel passionate about advocating for the rights of marginalized people groups such as racial minorities, indigenous people, immigrants, incarcerated people, and women. According to *Christianity Today*, "the rising concern for justice is seen most dramatically among the younger generation... Communications, technology, travel opportunities, and the forces of globalization have meant that young people have had more exposure to the reality of suffering and injustice in our world than any previous generation."[123]

This "Justice" generation has access to human history at the touch of a button. Nothing is hidden anymore. The mistakes of the past have caught up with humanity, including the mistakes of the Christian church. Everyone knows that atrocities have been committed in the name of God. Previous constructs of history are being challenged.

This generation is fed up with injustice and hypocrisy. It will never be reached through religious traditionalism or perfunctory platitudes. It needs real, humble, authentic answers.

---

[122] n.d. https://www.pewresearch.org/fact-tank/2015/05/12/millenials-increasingly-are-driving-growth-of-nones/

[123] n.d. https://www.pewresearch.org/fact-tank/2015/05/12/millenials-increasingly-are-drivBethany Hoang, "The Justice Generation," Christianity Today, August 23, 2010, https://www.christianitytoday.com/pastors/2010/summer/justicegen.html

Colleges and Coffee shops

Public colleges and universities, once centers of Christian thought, have become hotbeds of skepticism and anti-religious dogma. One survey of over 1200 faculty members from 712 colleges and universities reported that "fifty-three percent of respondents admitted to harboring unfavorable feelings toward evangelicals." [124]

If you work or study in a secular environment, it's inevitable that people will question what you believe and why. You will likely be criticized for holding a biblical worldview. Sharing your faith in this type of environment is daunting. *But it's never been more important.* As renowned Christian author and apologist C.S. Lewis once wrote, "Good philosophy must exist, if for no other reason, because bad philosophy needs to be answered."[125]

The current state of affairs should leave us hopeful rather than discouraged. What a privilege to share the truth of God's love with people living in confusion. Like Esther, you are here "for such a time as this."[126] Sharing your faith will require brain power, heart power, and Holy Spirit power, but Jesus has promised to give you these things. So, without further ado, let's explore eight tips for effective apologetics.

1. Be Friendly!

People listen to those they like. If you want to build credibility and influence, look for ways to be kind, generous, and helpful to those

---

[124] Gary A. Tobin and Aryeh Kaufmann Weinberg, Political Beliefs & Behavior of College Faculty (San Francisco, CA: Institute For Jewish & Community Research, 2006).

[125] C.S. Lewis, The Weight of Glory and Other Addresses (London: William Collins, 2013).

[126] Esther 4:14

around you. As the old saying goes, "People don't care how much you know until they know how much you care."

I never would have agreed to study the Bible with my coworker and his family if I didn't know he had my best interest in mind. His friendly disposition and humble attitude did a lot to build my trust. Good apologists take time to understand the beliefs, values, and backgrounds of those they're trying to reach. Jesus taught the apostles to tailor their messages to the Gentiles differently than their messages to the Jews. Your content and communication style should match the interests, cultures, and educational levels of those you are trying to reach.

We should take care to be kind and humble when disagreeing with other people's viewpoints. It's never helpful to insult the intelligence of those we are talking with, or to speak disparagingly of people whose theories differ from our own. Truth speaks for itself. It doesn't need sarcasm or superiority as a sidekick.

2. Research, Research, Research!

Scripture says, *"The heart of the righteous studies how to answer"* (Proverbs 15:28).

If you want to share your faith with others, you need to know *why* you believe what you believe. Why do you believe in Scripture? What evidence can you share for the resurrection? How do you explain the problem of evil? Why do you think intelligent design is a legitimate explanation for origins? These are just a few of many important questions apologists can address.

It's essential to do your homework! Study the classic arguments for faith, and try to stay up to date with newly-emerging information.

Apologetics should be fun and fascinating. Is there an area of study you feel particularly interested in? *The arts? Natural science? Social science? Philosophy? Math? Logic? Music?* Each of these fields reveals something about God.

Try to discover how intelligent believers in your area of interest connect their field to *their faith*. Read their written works and grapple with their thought processes. What does your area of interest reveal about God and His creation?

I love philosophy, so I enjoy reading the works of Bible-believing philosophers. Great thinkers (such as Alvin Plantinga) amaze me with their command of language and their brilliant ability to weave their faith into their works. Scientists such as Hugh Ross (and the others listed in Chapter 3) see God's handiwork throughout nature.

You can use the arguments, struggles, defenses, and discoveries of great men and women of faith in your apologetics today.

3. Don't Stress

Many are hesitant to share their faith because they're afraid of all the things they don't know.

"What if I'm asked a question that catches me off guard?" you might wonder.

That's okay!

If you knew everything, *you would be God*. God doesn't need geniuses as much as He needs witnesses — people who can testify how they found Him in their lives and areas of study.

Imagine someone is building a house. To save money, the owner oversees the project himself, hiring various subcontractors. One expert lays the foundation, another does the electric wiring, and another the framing. Others come in to do the dry walling, finishing, plumbing, etc. Once the house is ready for inspection, the county inspector notices some flaws in the electric wiring. He gives the house a fail until the issues can be fixed.

Although the housing inspector has a general knowledge of construction, he doesn't need to be an expert in every aspect of it in order to know whether a house is safe. He just has to notice the flaws. Similarly, the apologist doesn't have to be an expert in every field. He or she simply needs to recognize some of the big issues at stake, notice some of the flaws in people's objections, and kindly offer an alternative.

Of course, you'll run into times when you simply don't know anything about a particular question or argument. Don't panic. Being honest and humble about your limitations can itself be a witness. When you're confronted with a difficult question, simply say: *"That's a great question. I have a few ideas, but I'm not entirely sure."* or *"That's a great question. I'd love to do some research on it so we can discuss this more."*

4. Be Mindful of Presuppositions

When a person has a negative concept of God, he or she inevitably has a faulty presupposition.

What's a presupposition?

According to the Oxford English Dictionary, a presupposition is *"a thing tacitly assumed beforehand at the beginning of a line of argument or course of action."*

When your coworker explains her cynicism about God, she's assuming certain things about the God she's rejecting. Perhaps she was raised to believe God was strict and demanding. Perhaps she was mistreated by a Christian leader. Perhaps someone close to her died and she didn't understand why God allowed it. Perhaps discussions about God and religion trigger feelings of fear, guilt, or anger.

There are plenty of reasons why someone might identify as an atheist which have little to do with science, logic, or math. Many apologetic arguments deal with topics outside the arena of personal human experience. It's important to discuss the rational basis for the resurrection, the case for intelligent design, the archaeological corroboration of Biblical events, etc. However, the emotional objections people have to faith are often stronger than their intellectual objections, whether they understand this or not.

If we share rational arguments without addressing emotional objections, we may actually reinforce people in the positions they've already taken. Apologists who are mindful of the human experience will try to keep their listener's presuppositions in mind. According to author and international speaker, Ty Gibson:

> "Presuppositional apologetics assumes the unbeliever already "knows" the truth of God's existence but is suppressing that truth by means of evasion techniques, such as rational argument, blame-casting, and obsessions or addictions that operate as masking maneuvers. Presuppositional apologetics *centers attention on the character of God* rather than on the existence of God and on the innate human experience, thus driving the conversation in the direction of the human being's vulnerability to love rather than arousing the ego in argument. 'Presuppositional apologetics' regards the revelation and witness of the character of God in

the Christian's beliefs, life, attitude, spirit, relief work, healing ministry, and justice advocacy, as the most persuasive evidence in favor of Christ. Love constitutes evidence. The 'argument' is *won* precisely because the goal is not to win an argument, but rather to win meaningful connection, respect and trust in the relationship. The rational mind follows wherever authentic love leads. Paraphrasing Jesus, 'They will know Me by your love.'" [127]

Presuppositional apologetics addresses assumptions people have within their beliefs.

At times, the best apologetic approach is simply to sit down and listen to people. You might be surprised to find yourself resonating with their reasons for unbelief. Bad religion has produced many atheists and skeptics. These people deserve our kindness, respect, and compassion.

5. Identify Contradictions

Greg Bahnsen, my favorite presuppositional apologist once stated, "*They (atheists) are breathing God's air all the time they are arguing against him.*"[128] He was referring to the fact that atheists often inadvertently borrow Judeo-Christian terms and concepts in their attempts to discredit the notion of God. If you listen closely, you'll likely find that many of the statements people make against faith are self-contradictory. The logic of these statements crumbles under close scrutiny.

---

[127] Ty Gibson, "[Tweets Re: Presuppositional Apologetics]," Twitter, October 12, 2020, https://twitter.com/tyfgibson/status/1315671893735804930.

[128] Greg L. Bahnsen and Joel Mcdurmon, Presuppositional Apologetics: Stated and Defended (Powder Springs, GA: American Vision, Inc., 2008).

Here are a few examples:

1. There is no truth... (*If it's true that there's no truth, then isn't there truth?*)
2. You can't know truth... (*If this statement is true, then don't you know truth?*)
3. No one has the truth... (*If this statement is true, don't you have the truth?*)
4. All truth is relative... (*Except for this statement about truth?*)
5. It's true for you but not for me... (*Does truth change depending on who believes it?*)
6. There are no absolutes... (*Isn't that an absolute?*)
7. You can't know anything for sure... (*Are you sure?*)
8. You should doubt everything... (*Should I doubt your suggestion to doubt everything?*)
9. Only science can give us truth... (*So you do believe ultimate truth exists?*)
10. You shouldn't judge my atheism... (*Is this statement a judgment?*)
11. People should keep beliefs about morality to themselves... (*Isn't that a moral belief?*)
12. God doesn't take sides... (*Does He take the sides of people who don't think He takes sides?*)
13. You shouldn't try to change people's beliefs... (*Aren't you trying to change my beliefs?*)
14. You should be tolerant of all views... (*Can you be tolerant of my desire to find truth?*)
15. It's arrogant to claim to have the truth... (*Are you claiming that this statement is true?*)

Note: The "responses" listed here are not intended to be verbatim replies, but are written to help the reader see the flaws in the logic of such statements.

Self-defeating statements are often provided as actual reasons for unbelief. As impassioned as the person making such comments may be, these statements are illogical. As proponents of biblical faith, we are also proponents of all that is true. Many times, when people begin to recognize the inherent contradictions of fallacious thoughts such as the ones listed above, they become more open to the pervasiveness of truth itself.

Of course, we should be kind and tactful when pointing out the flaws in other people's thinking. It may be best to remain silent when someone is irritated or unwilling to listen.

The theory of Determinism is fueled by self-defeating argumentation. Determinists teach that all systems of life operate by logical mechanisms outside of human control. They deny the existence of free will, volition, and human freedom. If determinism is true, you aren't reading this chapter because you chose to, but because of a complex cascade of biological events completely out of your control. Even your own thoughts are a series of chemical reactions.

Here's why this theory is self-defeating:

1) Determinists believe their claims are rational. However, to be rational, a belief must be freely chosen, and freely processed. According to Determinism, however, this is impossible.

2) Determinists claim it's impossible to make statements about what is ultimately true since even these statements will be determined by pre-existing mechanisms and chemical reactions. However, to claim that Determinism is the real truth violates this very principle.

3) In their debates, Determinists try to change people's minds about the nature of reality. However, determinism itself teaches that changes of opinion occur from chemical reactions, not from argumentation.

Determinism sounds compelling to some, but a closer look reveals how self-defeating it is. As you dialogue with Determinists, listen for these self-defeating statements and try to respectfully help others recognize them.

6. Question the Questioner

Jesus used the art of questioning to disarm people's prejudice. Luke's gospel tells the story of Jesus coming to Jerusalem as a young boy. Missing in action, Jesus was eventually found dialoguing with the Jewish priests and scholars in the temple, much to the chagrin of his parents.

> "Now so it was that after three days they found Him in the temple, sitting in the midst of the teachers, both listening to them and asking them questions. And all who heard Him were astonished at His understanding and answers." (Luke 2:46)

Imagine the scene. The young boy Jesus is surrounded by aged men who have studied for decades, memorized generous portions of Scripture, and fiercely debated spiritual topics. The very idea that a young boy would attempt to instruct Israel's spiritual elite would seem highly offensive, but Jesus knew how to disarm prejudices through the humble art of asking questions.

Through His questions, Jesus inquisitively drew responses from the priests while simultaneously challenging them to think deeply. While they thought they were teaching, *they were actually being taught*. Who knows what grand spiritual themes were presented by that curious young Man? The seeds of truth presented during that fantastic encounter very likely led some to accept Jesus when He began proclaiming the Kingdom of Heaven.

Jesus continued to use questions throughout His ministry. This wasn't a new technique, however. In the Old Testament, God often asked questions to Israel.

The word *question* comes from the root word, *quest*, or journey. Questions are designed to be a quest for answers. Good apologists ask good questions. This skill takes practice, but is well worth the effort. Through His questions, Jesus:

- revealed His divinity by His heart-searching words.
- gently exposed the misconceptions and assumptions of His questioners.
- discreetly pointed out prejudice and sin.
- instilled a desire for something more in the hearts of His listeners.

In college, I took a class on the philosophy of science. My professor dedicated the last month of class to critiquing religious notions of the origin of life. On the last day, she shared the National Academy of Science's criteria for real science. At the end, she asked for our thoughts.

I raised my hand and asked, *"Professor, one of the criteria you mentioned is that actual science must be testable or repeatable. Is that correct?"*

"Yes, that's correct!" she replied.

"How can you test the theory of macroevolution if what supposedly took place happened millions of years ago?" I asked.

Stepping away from the chalkboard, she said, *"Well, you would test the theory by seeing if macroevolution evidence can be found... in the fossil record, for example."*

"But is the fossil record continuous or discontinuous?" I asked.

All eyes looked my direction. The professor cleared her throat.

"Yes, that is true, the fossil record is discontinuous..." she said.

"In the last century, haven't several documented hoaxes been introduced into museums on behalf of paleontology?" I asked.

"Actually, that is very true," she replied. *"There were numerous cases in which the reconstruction of bone fossils was found to be inaccurate."*

Whispering a prayer, I decided to keep asking.

"Is it also true that the theory of macroevolution has been altered multiple times in order to address some of its inconsistencies? For example, the punctuated equilibrium idea was introduced to account for sudden changes in species?"

"That is correct," she said. *"That idea of rapid development took place to explain a lack of intermediary fossils."*

I asked her one more question: *"How many alterations does a theory need before it is finally dismissed?"*

With a slight smile and then a sigh, she said, *"I guess that's why we are here. To understand what science really is."* And with that, she ended the class.

Many of the students stayed to talk about this after class. Thankfully, my professor was very cordial toward me. She gave me an A and even affirmed my classroom contribution! I was grateful God had given me wisdom to know which questions to ask.

It's important to ask questions humbly in order to prevent unnecessary difficulties. These conversations are often sensitive for people. At the end of the day, apologists are trying to save souls, not to offend people. We want to draw people to the truth, not to repulse them by obnoxiously acting like we know everything.

The next chapter contains a variety of questions you can ask when trying to defend your faith. The best questions are designed to evoke honest, careful thought.

7. Tell Stories

Jesus was a master storyteller. The gospel of Mark says, "He did not say anything to them without using a parable. But when he was alone with his own disciples, he explained everything" (Mark 4:4). Stories can capture people's attention and communicate truths in ways that nothing else can. Try to find ways to include stories in your apologetics. Most importantly, don't be afraid to share the story of what God's done for you.

8. Share the Big Picture

In 1 Corinthians 9, the great apologist Paul shared his secret to "win as many as possible." He said, "I have become all things to all people so that by all possible means I might save some." Paul meant that that with every group of people he tried to reach, he found as much common ground with them as possible in order to build their trust. This technique is apparent in Paul's preaching. His sermons and letters varied depending on who he was addressing, what their background was, and what prejudices they had.

Apologists need to follow this example. Not all of our listeners will believe in God or Scripture. Using multiple Bible verses to prove a point may backfire. Biblical vocabulary, sometimes called *"Christianese,"* can sound like a foreign language.

How can you best help these people?

Learn to articulate the big reasons why you believe what you do — the philosophical, yet simple explanations behind your beliefs. For example, if you're trying to explain a Biblical doctrine, such as the second coming of Jesus, ask yourself, *"What's the big idea behind this?"*

The second coming is not just about the signs of the times, the apocalypse, or how to prepare for the end of the world. *The big idea is that God is coming to put an end to suffering and take His people home.*

Big ideas are simple and elegant. They explain the *"why"* behind Biblical truths, pointing to the greatest truth of all — God's love.

Here are a few big picture ideas:
- Why do the ten commandments matter? *"Because God wants us to live an abundant life of love."*
- What is the goal of salvation? *"God wants you to be eternally healthy, connected, and happy."*
- Why is the Sabbath relevant? *"God loves you and wants to spend time with you."*
- What is the purpose of Scripture? *"God has given us a love letter to help us in this life and guide us to the next."*
- How can we make sense of hell? *"It's not what most people think it is. God's temporary justice is designed to put an end to evil, forever."*
- Why is grace necessary? *"It removes guilt and shame, improving our relationships with ourselves, others, and God."*

Sharing the *why* of your beliefs will help people understand that your faith isn't blind faith, but *reasonable* faith. This approach will highlight the most significant truth of all – God's infinite love.

The *essence* of the apologetic task is to paint a beautiful picture of God.

If you're an apologist, you're an artist.

THINKING ABOUT APOLOGETICS:

- Has anyone explained to you why they don't believe in God? If so, how did you respond? What would you say to them now?

- What are some of the unique needs of young people today?

- The apostle Peter wrote, "Always be prepared to give an answer [apologia] to everyone who asks you to give the reason for the hope that you have. But do this with gentleness and respect."[129] Why are gentleness and respect so important to apologetics?

- What's an example of a self-defeating statement?

- What's the big idea behind the resurrection of Christ?

---

[129] 1 Pet. 3:15

Chapter 10
Questioning the Questioner

Jesus understood the art of questioning.

According to Yale theologian Martin Copenhaver, the gospel accounts reveal that Jesus asked many more questions than He answered: *"Asking questions was central to Jesus' life and teachings. In fact, for every question he answers directly he asks—literally—a hundred."* [130]

The best teachers know that asking the right questions will help engage student's minds more than acting like an expert could ever. When learning new concepts, people need to be part of the discovery process. This requires curiosity. In the words of the late author Nancy Willard, "Answers are closed rooms, and questions are open doors that invite us in."[131]

---

[130] Martin B. Copenhaver, Jesus Is the Question: The 307 Questions Jesus Asked and the 3 He Answered (Nashville, TN: Abingdon Press, 2014).

[131] Nancy Willard, Telling Time: Angels, Ancestors, and Stories (Open Road Media, 2014).

Of course, answers are still very important. We've looked at many answers in this book. But the best apologists try to ask the right questions in order to motivate people to seek answers. That was the method of Jesus – the best apologist of all.

Below are a variety of questions you can ask when dialoguing with others about their beliefs. You can choose which questions might be relevant for the person you're talking to, and modify them to match your own communication style. This list is by no means exhaustive, but I hope it will help you share some of the things you've learned in this book.

Apologetics:

- Can you define apologetics?
- Do you think we need apologetics? Why or why not?
- Do you think most people have intelligent reasons for their faith? If not, why not?
- Are you aware of the history of Christian apologetics, such as in the early church?
- Do you think God wants us to bypass our brains to understand biblical themes?
- Have some people left the faith because things weren't properly explained to them?
- Have you examined some of the most compelling arguments for the Christian faith (intelligent design, the reliability of Scripture, the basis of morality, the problem of evil, etc.)?
- Would you like me to share why I believe faith is reasonable and rational?

Atheism:

- How did you become an atheist?
- Can you help me understand why you don't believe in God?

- Without God, where do you get your standard of morality?
- What, if anything, would change your mind about God?
- How can you explain the human longing for meaning and purpose, or inner thoughts such as, *Why do I feel unfulfilled or empty?*
- If God doesn't exist, how will the problem of evil and suffering ever be solved? How can people find hope or meaning in the midst of their suffering?
- Why does something exist rather than nothing?
- How do you explain the origins of the universe? What evidence led you to those conclusions?
- From your perspective, how do your beliefs differ from mine?

Origins:

- Do you think math is a human construct? Why or why not?
- Have you ever wondered why the same orderly mathematical patterns appear throughout our world? Could this suggest intelligent design?
- Our universe is incredibly fine-tuned to support life. Have you examined the probability that life on earth developed through evolutionary methods? Would you like me to share some of the numbers with you?
- If Genesis is figurative, then is the fall of man also figurative? What about salvation? Some Christians have embraced theistic evolution, but doesn't this teaching undermine Scripture and faith in general?
- The Bible teaches that God is love, describing His original creation as "very good." Why would a good God use evolution, a process that involves death, suffering, and domination (survival of the fittest) to create our world?
- If God used evolution to slowly create life over millions of years, death and suffering must have been part of his

original plan. Why then would He want to put an end to suffering by creating a new heavens and earth?
- If the Genesis creation account isn't literal, how do you explain the creation language used many other places in Scripture, including the New Testament?[132] (Exodus 20:8-11, Mark 10:6-8, John 1:1-4, Revelation 14:7, etc.)
- As I understand it, there's no purpose or ultimate meaning in evolution. How do you reconcile this fact with the purposes of God? Why would God be necessary in an evolutionary world?
- If, as some evolutionists claim, dinosaurs lived and died thousands of years before Adam, how do we explain Romans 5:12-15, which states that Adam's sin brought death into the world?
- Do you ever consider the remarkable beauty of nature and wonder, even for a moment, if a Designer is behind it all? Did you know Darwin wondered this at times?

Scripture:

- What are the criteria used to determine whether a historical document is accurate?
- Plato wrote about Socrates. How do we judge whether Socrates existed?
- What piece of ancient literature has more ancient manuscripts than any other work?
- What Scriptures did Jesus use? (This is an argument in favor of the Old Testament).
- How do you account for the extensive archaeological documentation of real people, places, and events in Scripture?

---

[132] Ekkehardt Mueller, "Creation in the New Testament," Journal of the Adventist Theological Society 15, no. 1 (2004): 47–62, https://www.southern.edu/administration/academic-administration/docs/faculty/service/CreationintheNewTestament-byEkkehardtMueller.pdf

- How do you account for the millions of people who have been transformed by reading the Bible?
- Have you ever read the gospels?

The Problem of Evil:

- If you were in charge of the universe, how would you solve the problem of suffering? Could you change people's hearts without violating their choices?
- In order to question evil, don't you need a moral standard to define right and wrong? Where do you get that standard from?
- Throughout human history, many people have been treated unfairly. If God doesn't exist, is there any hope of future justice? Where does justice come from?
- If the evolutionary notion of "survival of the fittest," is true, why does authentic generosity and philanthropy exist? Why do we admire those who put others before themselves?
- What risk did God take in order to make humans and angels capable of love?
- Would you like to live in a world in which the possibility of evil didn't exist? What would the pros and cons be?

Genocide in the Bible:

- By what standard do you judge God to be immoral? What objective marker do you use?
- Is evil wrong? Are murder, rape, and theft wrong? If so, where does the universal standard of right and wrong come from?
- If God's Word and God's law are irrelevant, who gets to decide what's right or wrong? Why is this problematic?
- Is it possible to condemn the Holocaust without objective moral values?

- What do you know about the context of the Old Testament conquests? Do you think the context matters?
- What do you think about the just war theory? Do you think it was right or wrong for the Allied forces to intervene to stop Hitler?
- Have you considered God's potential motivations for the Old Testament conquests? These motivations likely include His desire to end human sacrifice, protect the lineage of the Messiah, and protect His people from violence, disease, idolatry, and prostitution.
- Do you believe there's more to the story than we currently understand?
- Do you think all who have died in judgment will be lost?

Abraham and Other Nations:

- What do you think Jesus meant when He claimed to be the "light of the world"?
- How many people do you think God wants to reach?
- Can you think of some creative ways God has communicated with people in the past?
- How do you account for the numerous stories in the Old Testament that describe God's efforts to save people who were not Jews. The New Testament also reveals God's heart to save Gentiles (and unbelievers from every nation).
- Read Romans 2:14-15. How do you explain this?

Chapter 11
The Greatest Apologetic

Do you believe in Bigfoot?

Ummmm ...

Believe it or not, several museums are dedicated to the alleged existence of this giant, hairy, ape-like creature. Bigfoot lurks anonymously in the backwoods of North America – or so the story goes.

I actually visited a Bigfoot museum a few years ago. While attending a Christian conference, my friend and I decided to check out the local town landmarks. Naturally, the museum piqued our curiosity.

Although I hadn't searched the far recesses of the North American wilderness, I didn't have a strong opinion about the existence or nonexistence of Bigfoot. However, after visiting the museum, *I became more of an unbeliever.*
Here's why:

Upon our arrival, my friend and I were greeted by a gigantic wooden carving of a Sasquatch (aka Bigfoot). As we entered the small center, we were immediately accosted by the smell of marijuana. We saw all sorts of Bigfoot paraphernalia—everything from footprint casts to fuzzy "photographs" of Bigfoot known as *blobsquatches*.

The owner of the museum (who is also the tour guide) told us dramatic tales of encountering the immense creatures himself. That's right, there is allegedly more than one Bigfoot (should they be called Bigfeet?).

The owner claimed that many people who had encountered Bigfoot refused to speak out for fear of ridicule.

Then it got weird. *Really weird.*

The man described his suspicion that these creatures were alien prisoners dropped off on our planet. He explained that the animals used special portals to evade curious hunters. He also thought it was possible that Bigfoot was half-angelic. The longer he talked, the stranger his explanations became.

As he shared, I thought to myself, *I've never believed in Bigfoot less than I do right now.*

For me, the biggest hindrance to believing in the existence of Bigfoot was, sometimes, Bigfoot believers themselves.

Could the same thing be true about God?

Perhaps the biggest hindrance to faith in the God of humanity could be the very humans claiming to represent Him. The representations, caricatures, portrayals, and pictures of God presented by Christians often actually deter people from Him.

People struggle with their picture of God for two reasons:
1) Not knowing any believers
2) Knowing certain kinds of believers

That's an unpopular opinion, but the same was true about Jesus' disciples early in their ministry. The gospel accounts reveal the disciple's anger towards the Romans, prejudice against the Samaritans, mistaken zeal in defending Jesus, and hostility toward those not following their methodology.

If the disciples, in their humanity, made mistakes, you can be sure that many Christians will today as well. Thankfully, God is merciful, patient, and kind. He finds ways to use us despite our mistakes.

Eventually, Christ's disciples discovered the power of love. Where words fail, love does not. The greatest apologetic has always been and will always be love.

In the words of one apologist: "The strongest argument in favor of the gospel is a loving and lovable Christian." [133]

The greatest defense of God's truth has always been a life of love for others.

Love is the universal language that needs no translation. Think about it. Four gospel accounts each describe the life and death of Jesus Christ. These accounts contain more stories of Jesus healing and advocating for people than of preaching to them. Describing the ministry of Jesus, one commentator wrote:

---

[133] Ellen G. White, The Ministry of Healing (Indo-European Publishing, 2019). Pg470

"Christ's method alone will give true success in reaching the people. The Savior mingled with people as one who desired their good. He showed sympathy for them, ministered to their needs, and won their confidence. Then He invited them, 'Follow Me.'"[134]

Love can include words, but should extend far beyond them. The most effective apologetic transcends words and arguments. Being courteous to those who disagree with us, tenaciously loving the "unlovable," going the extra mile for people, generously sharing our resources, and refusing to give up on others — these actions speak more powerfully on behalf of Jesus than all the oration and lectures of the greatest Christian philosophers.

This might explain why Paul the Apostle claimed that *"Love never fails."* [135]

When I first became a Christian, I heard people at church talking about the "love chapter" in the Bible. They were referring to 1 Corinthians 13 where Paul elaborates on the qualities of love. They assumed I knew what they were talking about, but I didn't.

In an attempt to find this "love chapter," I searched for "love" in the Bible and found multiple references in John's epistles. John's writings speak of love more than any other New Testament books. In John's epistles, the words "God" and "love" are frequently used together. To John, he could not talk about love without talking about God... and he could not talk about God, without talking about love. To him, God and Love were inexorably bound.

John didn't just say that God was loving, He said "God is love." [136]

---

[134] Ibid 73.4

[135] 1 Cor. 13:8

> *It's impossible to speak of God's existence without also speaking of His heart.*

This point shouldn't escape us so quickly. God's people will misrepresent him unless genuine love flows through their words and actions.

The Bible teaches that fallen humanity is the object of God's special care and affection. God has demonstrated His infinite love for us in the gift of His Son.

In Jesus, heaven gave everything.

Jesus would have died for you even if you were the only person on the planet. He would have done it even if you ultimately chose to reject him, simply in order to give you a chance. Regardless of your present situation or past history, you are deeply and perfectly loved.

God's love is worth experiencing *and* sharing.

According to Bible prophecy, we're living in unprecedented times, probably much closer to the end of time than we suspect. The war between good and evil is wrapping up. People are making decisions that will impact their eternal destinies. Remarkable blessings await us.

God wants to use each of us to encourage others toward the kingdom of heaven. As we attempt to share the love of Christ, our apologetics will witness to His truth and goodness. There's nothing more meaningful than helping others understand God's Word and His love more clearly.

---

[136] 1 Jn. 4:8

...The world court case continues.

The lawyers make their arguments.

The jury watches in rapt silence.

The witnesses rise one after another.

And then ...

"Your Honor, I call to the stand as my witness, _____."

Your name is called.

It may not be a literal court you're called to. It may be a classroom, an office, a coffee shop, or a bus stop. But it's your turn to share.

You're up.

Each and every day, you have opportunities to reveal God's goodness and truth to the people around you. These divine appointments carry tremendous potential. God wants to use you to impact eternity.

Are you ready?

This is apologetics.

ACKNOWLEDGMENTS

A special thanks to all my friends and family who helped with this project. I'm very grateful for my editors, proofreaders, soundboards, prayer warriors, professors, and everyone else who contributed.

David Asscherick
Elise Harboldt
Kerstin Ashby Ferguson
Brian Simmons
Shenalyn Page
Rosemary Andrykanus
(Late) V. Bailey Gillespie
Savonna Greer

Thank you again.

NOTES

1. Aguirre, Anthony. "Multiverse | Definition, Types, & Facts." In Encyclopedia Britannica, December 19, 2018. https://www.britannica.com/science/multiverse.

2. "An Introduction to the Book of Job." bible.org, n.d. https://bible.org/article/introduction-book-job.

3. Bahnsen, Greg L., and Joel McDurmon. Presuppositional Apologetics: Stated and Defended. Powder Springs, GA: American Vision, Inc., 2008.

4. Barton, John How the Bible came to be (Louisville, KY: Westminster John Knox press, 1998), 85.

5. Berlinski, David. 2008. The Devil's delusion: atheism and its scientific pretensions. New York: Crown Forum.

6. Berry, George R. "The Ethical Teaching of the Old Testament." The Biblical World 21, no. 2 (1903): 108-14. Accessed April 29, 2021.

7. Bracey, John, and John Hope Franklin. "Race and History: Selected Essays, 1938-1988." The Journal of American History 77, no. 2 (September 1990): https://doi.org/.

8. British Humanist Association. "The Bus Campaign," February 20, 2012.

9. Bruce, F. F. The New Testament Documents: Are They Reliable?. Grand Rapids, MI: Eerdmans, 1974.

10. Celizic, Mike. "Families Speak about Switched Identity Ordeal." MSNBC, March 27, 2008. https://www.today.com/news/families-speak-about-switched-identity-ordeal-1C9015997.

11. Copan, Paul. Is God a Moral Monster?: Making Sense of the Old Testament God. Grand Rapids, MI: Baker Books, 2011.

12. Copenhaver, Martin B. Jesus Is the Question: The 307 Questions Jesus Asked and the 3 He Answered. Nashville, TN: Abingdon Press, 2014.

13. Darwin, Charles, and Francis Darwin. Charles Darwin: His Life Told in an Autobiographical Chapter, and in a Selected Series of His Published Letters. London: John Murray, 1908.

14. Davies, P. C. W. Cosmic jackpot: Why our universe is just right for life. Boston: Houghton Mifflin, 2007.

15. Dawkins, Richard. The God Delusion. London Black Swan, 2016.

16. Diodorus, Siculus, and Francis R. Walton. Diodorus of Sicily: Fragments of Books XXI - XXXII. Cambridge, MA: Harvard Univ. Press, 1980.

17. Dr. Robert Kurland. "23 Famous Scientists Who Are Not Atheists." Magis Center, May 19, 2019. https://magiscenter.com/23-famous-scientists-who-are-not-atheists/.

18. Flew, Antony, and Gary Habermas. "My Pilgrimage from Atheism to Theism." Philosophia Christi 6, no. 2 (2004): 197–211. https://doi.org/10.5840/pc20046224.

19. Frail, T. A. "Meet the 100 Most Significant Americans of All Time." Smithsonian Magazine, n.d. https://www.smithsonianmag.com/smithsonianmag/meet-100-most-significant-americans-all-time-180953341/?no-ist.

20. Gamble, Dave (25 May 2014). "Antony Flew – did he really change his mind?". Skeptical-Science.com.

21. Garrett, Don. Nature and Necessity in Spinoza's Philosophy. New York, NY: Oxford University Press, 2018.

22. Geisler, Norman L. Christian Apologetics. Grand Rapids, MI: Baker Book House, 2013.

23. Gibson, Ty. "[Tweets Re: Presuppositional Apologetics]." Twitter, October 12, 2020. https://twitter.com/tyfgibson/status/1315671893735804930.

24. "God vs. Atheism: Is Atheism Logical?" Christian Research Institute, March 13, 2009. https://www.equip.org/perspectives/god-vs-atheism-is-atheism-logical/.

25. Hawking, Stephen, Eddie Redmayne, Kip S. Thorne, and Lucy Hawking. 2020. Brief Answers to the Big Questions. London, England: John Murray.

26. Hoang, Bethany. "The Justice Generation." Christianity Today, August 23, 2010. https://www.christianitytoday.com/pastors/2010/summer/justicegen.html.

27. Hobrink, Ben. Modern Science in the Bible: Amazing Scientific Truths Found in Ancient Texts. New York: Howard Books, 2011.

28. Hoyle, Fred. "The Universe: Past and Present Reflections." Annual Review of Astronomy and Astrophysics 20, no. 1 (September 1982): 8–12. https://doi.org/10.1146/annurev.aa.20.090182.000245.

29. "Ignoring Genocide (HRW Report - Leave None to Tell the Story: Genocide in Rwanda, March 1999)." hrw.org, 2019. https://www.hrw.org/reports/1999/rwanda/Geno15-8-01.htm.

30. J. Warner Wallace. God's Crime Scene: A Cold-Case Detective Examines the Evidence for a Divinely Created Universe. Colorado Springs, CO: David C. Cook, 2015.

32. Jenkins, Robert, and University Of St. Andrews. Library. Copyright Deposit Collection. The Reasonableness and Certainty of the Christian Religion. 2nd ed. London: W.B. for Richard Sare, 1708.

32. Joshua Ryan Butler. The Skeletons in God's Closet: The Mercy of Hell, the Surprise of Judgment, the Hope of Holy War. Nashville, TN: Thomas Nelson, 2014.

33. Justin, Brierley. "A Universe from Nothing? Lawrence Krauss & Rodney Holder." Unbelievable, June 23, 2014. https://unbelievable.podbean.com/e/a-universe-from-nothing-lawrence-krauss-rodney-holder-unbelievable-28-apr-2012/.

34. Keas, Mike. "Richard Weikart on the Revealing Inconsistencies of Scientific Materialism." Evolution News, April 18, 2016. https://evolutionnews.org/2016/04/richard_weikart_2/.

35. Kim, Theodore. "Case of Mistaken Identity Stuns Families." USA Today, June 1, 2006. https://usatoday30.usatoday.com/news/nation/2006-05-31-indiana-mistaken-identity_x.htm.

36. "Knot Theory." In Encyclopedia Britannica, 2019. https://www.britannica.com/science/knot-theory.

37. Kohl, Marvin. Infanticide and the Value of Life. Buffalo, NY: Prometheus Books, 1978.

38. Kreeft, Peter. "The Problem of Evil." www.peterkreeft.com, October 27, 2016. https://www.peterkreeft.com/topics/evil.htm.

39. Kreeft, Peter, and Ronald K. Tacelli. Pocket Handbook of Christian Apologetics. Downers Grove, Ill.: Intervarsity Press, 2003.

40. Lewis, C.S. Mere Christianity. New York, NY: Simon & Schuster, 1996.

41. The Great Divorce. London: Collins, 2012.

42. The Weight of Glory and Other Addresses. London: William Collins, 2013.

43. Lial, Margaret L., Charles D. Miller, and E. John Hornsby. Beginning Algebra: Student's Study Guide. New York, NY: Harper Collins Publishers, 1992.

44. Lipka, Michael. "7 Key Changes in the Global Religious Landscape." Pew Research Center, April 2, 2015. https://www.pewresearch.org/fact-tank/2015/04/02/7-key-changes-in-the-global-religious-landscape/.

45. Mangalwadi, Vishal. The Book That Changed Your World: How the Bible Created the Soul of Western Civilization. Nashville, TN, 2011.

46. Mariottini, Claude. "Canaan in Patriarchal Times – Part 1." Dr. Claude Mariottini, November 9, 2006. https://claudemariottini.com/2006/11/09/canaan-in-patriarchal-times-part-1/.

47. McDowell, Sean. "How Can God and Satan Be in a Cosmic Struggle?" Sean McDowell, n.d. https://seanmcdowell.org/blog/how-can-god-and-satan-be-in-a-cosmic-struggle.

48. Merriam-Webster. Merriam Webster's Collegiate Dictionary. Springfield, IL: Merriam-Webster, 2014.

49. Meyer, Stephen C. Signature in the Cell: DNA and the Evidence for Intelligent Design. New York, NY: Harperone, 2010.

50. Mishra, Sundar. "Land of Contradictions." Social Watch, 2018. https://www.socialwatch.org/node/10624.

51. Mueller, Ekkehardt. "Creation in the New Testament." Journal of the Adventist Theological Society 15, no. 1 (2004): 47–62. https://www.southern.edu/administration/academic-administration/docs/faculty/service/CreationintheNewTestament-byEkkehardtMueller.pdf.

52. Murray, Michael J. "The Problem of Evil in Early Modern Philosophy." Leibniz Society Review 12 (2002): 103–6. https://doi.org/10.5840/leibniz20021211.

53. Mykytiuk., Lawrence. "53 People in the Bible Confirmed Archaeologically." Biblical Archaeology Society, April 12, 2017. https://www.biblicalarchaeology.org/daily/people-cultures-in-the-bible/people-in-the-bible/50-people-in-the-bible-confirmed-archaeologically/.

54. Orr, James. International Standard Bible Encyclopedia, Vol. 1. Grand Rapids, Michigan: Wm. B. Eerdmans Pub. Co, 2003.

55. Owen, H. P., Concepts of Deity, London: Macmillan, 1971.

56. Pasachoff, Naomi E.; Littman, Robert J. (2005). A Concise History of the Jewish People. Lanham: Rowman & Littlefield. p. 154

57. P. C. W. Davies. Cosmic Jackpot: Why Our Universe Is Just Right for Life. Boston, MA: Houghton Mifflin, 2007.

58. Penrose, Roger. The Road to Reality: A Complete Guide to the Laws of the Universe. New York, NY: Vintage Books, Cop, 2007.

59. Pharyngula, N.P. "Science Blogs," April 29, 2013.

60. Pheme Perkins. Reading the New Testament: An Introduction. New York, NY: Paulist Press, 2012.

61. Plutarch. De Superstitione. Milano: Cisalpino-Goliardica, 1980.

62. Procter, Paul. Cambridge International Dictionary of English. Cambridge: Cambridge University Press, 1995.

63. Prothero, Stephen R. God Is Not One: The Eight Rival Religions That Run the World, and Why Their Differences Matter. Collingwood, Vic.: Black Inc., 2011.

64. "Reasons to Believe: Design and the Anthropic Principle," April 29, 2013.

65. Rhodes, Ron. Answering the Objections of Atheists, Agnostics, & Skeptics. Eugene, Or.: Harvest House Publishers, 2006.

66. Samples, Kenneth R. Without a Doubt: Answering the 20 Toughest Faith Questions. Grand Rapids, MI: Baker Books, 2004.

67. Schroder, Tim. "The Protein Puzzle," n.d. https://www.mpg.de/11447687/W003_Biology_medicine_054-059.pdf.

68. Schubart, Wilhelm. Papyri Graecae Berolinenses. Berlin, Germany: Marcus and Weber, 1911.

69. Shakespeare, William. Macbeth. Cambridge, UK: Cambridge University Press, 2012.

70. Spiegel, James S. The Making of an Atheist: How Immorality Leads to Unbelief. Chicago, IL: Moody Publishers, 2010.

71. Sproul, R.C. Defending Your Faith: An Introduction to Apologetics. Wheaton, IL: Crossway, 2003.

72. Stager, Lawrence. "Child Sacrifice in Carthage: Religious Rite or Population Control?" Journal of Biblical Archeological Review 10, no. 1 (January 1984): 31–46.

73. Steup, Matthias. The Stanford Encyclopedia of Philosophy: Epistemology. Edited by Edward N. Zalta. Spring 2014., 2005.

74. T. Edward Damer. Attacking Faulty Reasoning: A Practical Guide to Fallacy-Free Arguments. Boston, MA: Wadsworth, Cengage Learning, 2013.

75. The Holy Bible. New King James Version. Nashville, TN: Thomas Nelson, 1991.

76. Tobin, Gary A., and Aryeh Kaufmann Weinberg. Political Beliefs & Behavior of College Faculty. San Francisco, CA: Institute For Jewish & Community Research, 2006.

77. Geisler, Norman L., and Frank Turek. 2004. I don't have enough faith to be an atheist. Wheaton, Ill: Crossway Books.

78. Weber, Alfred. History of Philosophy. Translated by Frank Thilly. London Longmans, Green, 1914.

79. Weikart, Richard. The Death of Humanity: And the Case for Life. Washington, D.C.: Regnery Faith, 2016.

80. White, Ellen G. "Prophet or Not?" Ellen G White Truth, n.d. https://www.ellengwhitetruth.com.

81. The Desire of Ages: The Conflict of the Ages Illustrated in the Life of Christ,. Mountain View, CA, Portland, OR: Pacific Press Pub. Association, 1947.

82. The Ministry of Healing. Indo-European Publishing, 2019.

83. The Story of Patriarchs and Prophets: As Illustrated in the Lives of Holy Men of Old. Mountain View, CA: Pacific Press Pub. Assoc., 1958.

84. The Story of Prophets and Kings as Illustrated in the Captivity and Restoration of Israel. Mountain View, CA: Pacific Press Publishing, 1917.

85. Wigner, Eugene P. "The Unreasonable Effectiveness of Mathematics in the Natural Sciences. Richard Courant Lecture in Mathematical Sciences Delivered at New York University, May 11, 1959." Communications on Pure and Applied Mathematics 13, no. 1 (February 1960): 1–14. https://doi.org/10.1002/cpa.3160130102.

86. Willard, Nancy. Telling Time: Angels, Ancestors, and Stories. Open Road Media, 2014.

87. Wilson, Edward O. Consilience: The Unity of Knowledge. New York, NY: Knopf, 1998.